Register Your Book
at ibmpressbooks.com/ibmregister

Upon registration, we will send you electronic sample chapters from two of our popular IBM Press books. In addition, you will be automatically entered into a monthly drawing for a free IBM Press book.

Registration also entitles you to:

- Notices and reminders about author appearances, conferences, and online chats with special guests

- Access to supplemental material that may be available

- Advance notice of forthcoming editions

- Related book recommendations

- Information about special contests and promotions throughout the year

- Chapter excerpts and supplements of forthcoming books

Contact us

If you are interested in writing a book or reviewing manuscripts prior to publication, please write to us at:

Editorial Director, IBM Press
c/o Pearson Education
800 East 96th Street
Indianapolis, IN 46240

e-mail: IBMPress@pearsoned.com

Visit us on the Web: ibmpressbooks.com

Mainframe Basics for Security Professionals:

Getting Started with RACF®

Mainframe Basics for Security Professionals:

Getting Started with RACF®

Ori Pomerantz

Barbara Vander Weele

Mark Nelson

Tim Hahn

IBM Press
Pearson plc
Upper Saddle River, NJ • Boston • Indianapolis • San Francisco
New York • Toronto • Montreal • London • Munich • Paris • Madrid
Cape Town • Sydney • Tokyo • Singapore • Mexico City

Ibmpressbooks.com

IBM Press Program Managers: Tara Woodman, Ellice Uffer

Cover design: IBM Corporation

Associate Publisher: Greg Wiegand
Marketing Manager: Kourtnaye Sturgeon
Publicist: Heather Fox
Acquisitions Editor: Bernard Goodwin
Managing Editor: Gina Kanouse
Designer: Alan Clements
Project Editor: Anne Goebel
Copy Editor: Krista Hansing Editorial Services, Inc.
Indexer: Lisa Stumpf
Compositor: Nonie Ratcliff
Proofreader: Chelsey Marti
Manufacturing Buyer: Dan Uhrig

Published by Pearson plc
Publishing as IBM Press

This Book Is Safari Enabled

The Safari® Enabled icon on the cover of your favorite technology book means the book is available through Safari Bookshelf. When you buy this book, you get free access to the online edition for 45 days. Safari Bookshelf is an electronic reference library that lets you easily search thousands of technical books, find code samples, download chapters, and access technical information whenever and wherever you need it.

To gain 45-day Safari Enabled access to this book:

- Go to http://www.awprofessional.com/safarienabled
- Complete the brief registration form
- Enter the coupon code ZDFW-DULG-7PZL-XAGD-WESK

If you have difficulty registering on Safari Bookshelf or accessing the online edition, please e-mail customer-service@safaribooksonline.com.

Library of Congress Cataloging-in-Publication Data

Mainframe basics for security professionals : getting started with RACF / Ori Pomerantz ... [et al.].
 p. cm.
 ISBN 0-13-173856-9 (hardback : alk. paper) 1. z/OS. 2. Computer security. 3. Electronic digital computers. I. Pomerantz, Ori.
 QA76.9.A25M3138 2008
 004.16—dc22

                                    2007044290

   ISBN-13: 978-0-13-173856-0
   ISBN-10: 0-13-173856-9

Text printed in the United States on recycled paper at R.R. Donnelley in Crawfordsville, Indiana.
First printing December 2007

Contents

Foreword

Security—it comes in many forms in the IT world: physical security around a data center, user ID authentication when a transaction gets executed, access control against a database, audit records for anomaly detection. All these forms can be bought and paid for, yet, one element must be taught. That is, the human, the person who administers the security system, the person who operates a data center, the person who executes a transaction, or the person who moves data on tapes between buildings. Today there is so much personally identifiable data and so many chances for fraud that securing that information is critical to the global economy.

For more than 40 years, the IBM® mainframe has been the backbone of financial services and the retail industry. Billions of transactions are executed every day across this infrastructure. The mainframe is known for its rock-solid security and integrity, yet, that is possible only with the assurance of a well-trained staff operating those systems and ensuring that the essential processes are being adhered to.

UNIX® systems have become ubiquitous in the IT world as well. Universities train thousands of students on these systems annually. Most businesses with mainframe computers are operating UNIX systems as well. It is important that a consistent operational approach be taken across these systems, to maintain the security of the overall environment. This book is intended for administrators and systems programmers who have come from the UNIX world and attempts to explain the security nuances of the mainframe. Remarkably, although the syntax of commands might be completely different, a wealth of similarities exists in the operational environment. Based on its heritage and holistic design across the hardware, firmware, operating system, and middleware, the mainframe has some unique capabilities for additional security. This book looks at many of the basic and advanced properties for securing a mainframe, to help businesses maintain the integrity of their transactions.

The authors of this book have decades of experience in designing, developing, and operating mainframe security systems. They are experts in their field and have shared their knowledge to simplify the learning experience for the UNIX administrator who might be asked to step up to the management of mainframe security. I think you'll find this book to be a valuable addition toward gaining experience with the mainframe security model.

Jim Porell
IBM Distinguished Engineer
Chief Architect, System z™ Software
IBM

Preface

The reports of my death are greatly exaggerated.
—Mark Twain

Throughout the 1990s, many industry pundits predicted the demise of the mainframe. It seemed that the entire information technology (IT) industry got caught up in the frenzy of client/server this and distributed that. Some lost sight of the fact that the purpose of IT is to address business problems and opportunities. Many didn't realize that, during this time, the mainframe evolved substantially with the addition of a standardized UNIX® development and execution environment, web serving capabilities, Java™, XML support, TCP/IP, firewall, and virtualization, while continuing to grow in both standalone processing power and clustering capabilities. Of course, the mainframe also maintained its traditional strengths of reliability, availability, and security.

We are at a very interesting point in the continuing evolution of the mainframe: Regulatory pressures such as the Payment Card Industry (PCI) standards and Sarbanes-Oxley mandate that companies understand their data assets and protect them properly. Cooling and power costs are driving companies to consolidate their servers, to avoid the costs of building new facilities. The rapid multiplication of servers causes substantial growth in support and software costs. All of this together explains why many companies are taking a fresh look at the mainframe to expand both existing applications and new applications. Mainframes are not appropriate to every business need, but they are optimized for high-availability and I/O-intensive applications.

That growth in the use of the mainframe drives up the need for knowledgeable security administrators. This is where this book comes in. We assume that you are already an experienced security administrator on other systems, such as UNIX, Linux®, or Windows®. We also assume that you've never logged on to TSO, the z/OS® command-line interface.

This "nuts of bolts" book will teach you how to log on, work with the mainframe's TSO and ISPF (similar to a GUI for z/OS, except that it uses text and not graphics) interfaces, and perform the major tasks of a security administrator. We are very big believers in learning by doing. Hey, that's how *we* learned! Of course, going through the exercises requires you to have access to an actual mainframe.

Chapter 1, "Introduction to the Mainframe," teaches the historical background and the basics of using a mainframe. By the end of the chapter, you will be able to log on, allocate data sets and edit their members, run JCL jobs, use UNIX System Services, and access the documentation when you need it. UNIX System Services (USS) is a version of UNIX running under z/OS.

Chapter 2, "Users and Groups," teaches users and groups. By the end of the chapter, you will be able to create, modify, and delete users and groups.

Chapter 3, "Protecting Data Sets and Other Resources," teaches resource protection. This chapter teaches you how to manipulate the profiles that protect data sets (a term that covers the rough equivalents of files and directories), the profiles that protect other permissions, and the permissions for files and directories within USS.

Chapter 4, "Logging," teaches logging. You will learn how to configure the mainframe to log security events and how to generate reports that include only the relevant log entries.

Chapter 5, "Auditing," teaches auditing. You will learn about the main weaknesses that auditors look for and will learn how to use the standard auditing tools to find those weaknesses yourself and remedy them.

Chapter 6, "Limited-Authority RACF Administrators," teaches how to create limited-authority administrators when they are appropriate, and discusses their permissions. Your first mainframe security job is likely to be as a limited-authority administrator. Unlimited access, called `system-SPECIAL`, is usually reserved for a few senior security administrators in the mainframe environment.

Chapter 7, "Mainframes in the Enterprise-Wide Security Infrastructure," teaches how the mainframe integrates into the enterprise-wide security infrastructure. In contrast to the other chapters, this chapter is very theoretical. It explains what the enterprise-wide security infrastructure does and how it relates to the mainframe, but it does not include exercises.

Time to get started. Grab a cup of coffee, fire up your terminal emulator (we explain what that is in Chapter 1), and get started!

Acknowledgments

This book was so easy to write that it practically wrote itself. If you believe that, the authors have some ocean-front property in Arizona, Hungary, Chad, and Mongolia they would like to sell you, along with the Brooklyn Bridge and the Tower of London (pictured on the cover). The truth of the matter is that writing this book took a lot of effort, not all of it by the authors.

Jay Hill was the senior technical advisor, especially during the first phase of the book before Mark Nelson and Tim Hahn joined. Without him, this book would have never been conceived, let alone written.

Marie Vander Weele provided suggestions and guidance while helping us ensure that the material is accurate and easy to read. Her comments hugely improved this book for our readers, and we extend our thanks for her valuable contributions.

To our reviewers, **Daniel Craun, Mark Hahn, Nigel Pentland, Kevin See,** and **Dr. Frank Tate:** Without you, the book would have been a lot harder to write, a lot harder to read, and a lot closer to a work of fiction. Of course, any remaining errors are our own fault.

We couldn't have written this book without our editors, **Bernard Goodwin** and his assistant **Michelle Vincenti** from Prentice Hall, and **Bill Maloney** from IBM. We would also like to thank **Jim Porell** for his support during this project and for writing the foreword.

We thank **Teresa Pomerantz** for inspiring the title of this book. We found that we were too close to the solution to find a good title, and Teresa provided a much appreciated fresh perspective. Ori would also like to thank her for all the times she took care of the children on her own so he could write this, as well as for those children and being a wonderful wife in general.

About the Authors

Ori Pomerantz has been securing computer networks, and teaching other people to do the same, since 1995. Since joining IBM in 2003, he has written classes on various Tivoli® security products, including IBM Tivoli zSecure. He has a CISSP, and his expertise is security, not mainframes—just like the intended audience of this book.

Barbara Vander Weele is a software engineer at IBM Corp. As a part of IBM Worldwide Education, she has developed and presented education material for provisioning, security, storage, and business technologies. A University of Michigan graduate, Barbara began working in the IT industry in 1993 as a C++ programmer, converting legacy mainframe systems to Windows and UNIX applications. Since 2004, she has authored numerous education courses for IBM.

Mark Nelson, CISSP, is a Senior Software Engineer at IBM, a 20-year veteran of the RACF® Design team, and a frequent speaker on RACF and z/OS security-related topics. Mark's areas of expertise in RACF include logging and reporting, RACF database analysis, and DB2®. Mark's publications include *NaSPA Technical Support* magazine, *IBM Hot Topics,* the *zJournal,* and now this book!

Tim Hahn is a Distinguished Engineer at IBM and has been with IBM for 17 years. He is the Chief Architect for Secure Systems and Networks within the IBM Software Group Tivoli organization. He works on security product strategy, architecture, design, and development. Tim has worked on a variety of products in the past, including lead architecture, design, and development for the IBM Encryption Key Manager and the z/OS Security Server LDAP Server. Tim is currently working on encryption key management, W3C standards concerning end users' web experience, and integration of Tivoli Security products into end-to-end client deployment environments. Tim has published numerous articles discussing the use of Tivoli Security products in end-to-end deployment environments, and is a co-author of the book *e-Directories: Enterprise Software, Solutions, and Services.*

Introduction to the Mainframe

The mainframe is the backbone of many industries that are the lifeblood of the global economy. More mainframe processing power is being shipped now than has ever been shipped. Businesses that require unparalleled security, availability, and reliability for their "bet your business" applications depend on the IBM zSeries® mainframe, which runs the z/OS operating system and is protected by the IBM Resource Access Control Facility (RACF).

In this book, we explain the basics of z/OS, focusing on z/OS security and RACF. This chapter describes the evolution of the mainframe and the reasons it is the leading platform for reliable computing. It also explains how to use the key elements of z/OS.

1.1 Why Use a Mainframe?

This book introduces security administrators to the world of z/OS. We expect that you already have experience with Linux, UNIX, or Windows. Using this prerequisite knowledge, we teach you how to use the mainframe and how to configure RACF, the security subsystem. At the end of each chapter, we list sources for additional information.

If you are the kind of person who wants to go right to typing commands and seeing results, skip on over to Section 1.2, "Getting Started," to learn about the z/OS Time Sharing Option (TSO) environment. However, we recommend that you read the rest of this section to understand the mainframe design philosophy. Many of the differences between the mainframe and other operating systems only make sense if you understand the history and philosophy behind mainframes.

1.1.1 A Little History

Few industries have had the rapid, almost explosive growth that we have seen in the information technology industry. The term *computer* originally referred to people who did manual calculations. The earliest nonhuman computers were mechanical devices that performed mathematical computations. Mechanical devices evolved into vacuum tube devices, which, in turn, were replaced by transistorized computers, which were replaced by integrated circuit devices.

Where do mainframes fit in? The mainframes we use today date back to April 7, 1964, with the announcement of the IBM System/360™. System/360 was a revolutionary step in the development of the computer for many reasons, including these:

- System/360 could do both numerically intensive scientific computing and input/output intensive commercial computing.

- System/360 was a line of upwardly compatible computers that allowed installations to move to more powerful computers without having to rewrite their programs.

- System/360 utilized dedicated computers that managed the input/output operations, which allowed the central processing unit to focus its resources on the application.

These systems were short on memory and did not run nearly as fast as modern computers. For example, some models of the System/360 were run with 32K (yes, K, as in 1,024 bytes) of RAM, which had to accommodate both the application and the operating system. Hardware and software had to be optimized to make the best use of limited resources.

IBM invested $5 billion in the development of the System/360 product line. This was a truly "bet your company" investment. Five billion dollars represented more than one and a half times IBM's total 1964 gross revenue of $3.2 billion. To put it into perspective, given IBM's 2005 gross revenue of $91 billion, an equivalent project would be more than a $140 billion project!

The z/OS operating system that we are discussing here traces itself back to System/360. One of the operating systems that ran on System/360 was OS/360. One variant of OS/360 was MVT (multitasking with a variable number of tasks). When IBM introduced virtual memory with System/370™, the operating system was renamed to SVS (single virtual storage), recognizing that a single virtual address space existed for the operating system and all users. This was quickly replaced with a version of the operating system that provided a separate virtual address space for each user. This version of the operating system was called MVS™ (multiple virtual storage). Later, IBM packaged MVS and many of its key subsystems together (don't worry about what a subsystem is just now…we'll get to that later) and called the result OS/390®, which is the immediate predecessor to z/OS.

1.1.2 Why Are Mainframes Different?

Mainframes were designed initially for high-volume business transactions and, for more than 40 years, have been continually enhanced to meet the challenges of business data processing. No computing platform can handle a diversity of workloads better than a mainframe.

But aren't "insert-your-favorite-alternative-platform" computers cheaper/faster/easier to operate? The answer is: It all depends. A student who is composing his term paper does not have the same information needs as a bank that needs to handle millions of transactions each day, especially because the bank also needs to be able to pass security and accounting audits to verify that each account has the correct balance.

Mainframes aren't for every computing task. Businesses opt for mainframes and mainframe operating systems when they have large volumes of data, large transaction volumes, large data transfer requirements, a need for an extremely reliable system, or many differing types of workloads that would operate best if they were located on the same computer. Mainframes excel in these types of environments.

1.1.3 Mainframe vs. Client/Server

In a client/server architecture, multiple computers typically cooperate to do the same task. For example, in Figure 1.1 the application uses a Web server, a database server, and an LDAP server.

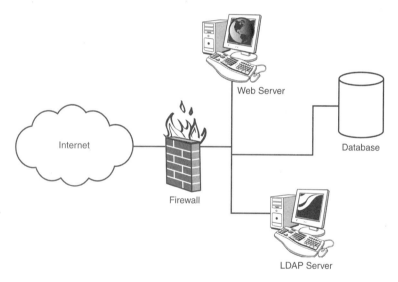

Figure 1.1 Client/server architecture

On a mainframe, the same computer does everything. One security package (RACF, in most cases) protects one operating system kernel. Mainframe subsystems do everything else, as you can see in Figure 1.2.

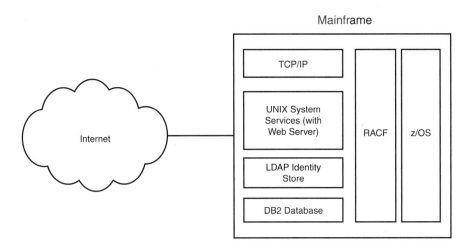

Figure 1.2   Mainframe architecture

That's a little of the "why" of mainframes. Now let's get started with the "how."

1.2 Getting Started

Virtually every computer book starts with a simple example that enables you to get your feet wet. We've got several "Hello, World" examples that will introduce you to:

1. Interactive computing using the z/OS Time Sharing Option (TSO)

2. Batch computing using Job Control Language (JCL)

3. UNIX System Services (USS)

1.2.1 What You Will Need

For the purposes of this chapter, you'll need a TSO and OMVS user ID for a z/OS system and the initial password. This user ID is created for you by a system administrator. Your user ID is a one- to seven-character string that is your "handle" for all the work you do within z/OS. It's the basis for your computer identity within z/OS and the anchor point for all your access control permissions.

For the other chapters of this book, you will need your own z/OS image, a copy of the operating system running inside its own virtual machine. On this image, you will need a TSO account with RACF special authority, which corresponds roughly to root under UNIX. Because you will need to change audit settings, it is not enough to have privileges for a specific group within RACF—you need to have global RACF special authority.

1.2.2 Logging in to the Mainframe

In the old days, access to the mainframe was handled mostly by dedicated terminals that were hard-wired to the mainframe. Today, the terminal is a run-of-the-mill PC connected by TCP/IP. The PC runs a program that imitates an old-fashioned terminal.

To connect to the mainframe, run the terminal emulator and point it to the IP address of the mainframe and the TCP port number for TSO. After you do that, you might need to "dial" to the correct virtual machine. Figure 1.3 shows a user "dialing" to NMP122, the z/OS 1.6 image used for the screenshots in this book. Some terminal emulators require you to press the right Ctrl key, instead of Enter, to enter a command to the mainframe; this is because the right Ctrl key is located where the Enter key was located on the original 3270 terminal. After you connect to the image, you might need to type **TSO <your user ID>** to reach the TSO logon panel.

```
          USE OF THIS SYSTEM IS FOR IBM MANAGEMENT APPROVED PURPOSES ONLY

     Fill in your USERID and PASSWORD (which will not appear) and press ENTER.
     If you are already logged on, enter LOGON userid HERE on the COMMAND line.
     USERID   ===>
     PASSWORD ===>

     COMMAND  ===> d nmp122_

                                                        RUNNING    RALVMR
```

Figure 1.3   The command to dial the correct system

Figure 1.4 shows the TSO logon panel. On this panel, enter the user ID that you've been given in (1) in the figure, your password in (2), and a new password of your choosing in (3). Because the person who created your user ID knows the password, you need to change it to ensure that, from now on, only you can log on to TSO using your user ID. Press Enter to start the logon process.

```
  ------------------------------ TSO/E LOGON ------------------------------------

     Enter LOGON parameters below:          RACF LOGON parameters:

     Userid    ===>  (1)

     Password  ===>  (2)  _                  New Password ===> (3)

     Procedure ===> GENERAL                  Group Ident  ===>

     Acct Nmbr ===> ACCT#
```

Figure 1.4   TSO logon panel

After a few moments, you'll see lines displayed that look similar to Figure 1.5. The first line tells you the last time your user ID was used. This is an elementary intrusion-detection mechanism: If the date and the time do not look correct, you should call your security department to investigate who is using your user ID without your permission.

```
ICH70001I ORIPOME  LAST ACCESS AT 17:44:08 ON FRIDAY, JANUARY 5, 2007
IKJ56455I ORIPOME LOGON IN PROGRESS AT 20:18:08 ON JANUARY 6, 2007
************************************************
* NMP122    This System is Running        *
*                  z/OS 1.6                *
*           Maintenance Level:  RSU0606    *
*                                          *
* IBM'S INTERNAL SYSTEMS MUST ONLY BE USED FOR *
* CONDUCTING IBM'S BUSINESS OR FOR PURPOSES   *
* AUTHORIZED BY IBM MANAGEMENT.'              *
*                                          *
* USE IS SUBJECT TO AUDIT AT ANY TIME BY IBM  *
* MANAGEMENT                               *
************************************************
READY
```

Figure 1.5   TSO logon results

The second line tells you how long you have until you will need to change your password. A good security policy requires that you change your password periodically. Your installation's policy is enforced whenever you enter the system.

The next line tells you that you have been authenticated (that is, your password is correct and you have not been denied access to the system for any other reason), and now TSO starts to build your logon environment.

This is followed by an installation-specific message, usually reminders of important aspects of your installation's information policy.

Some installations take users immediately into ISPF, the menu-driven system you will later see in Figure 1.8. In that case, type **=x** to exit into TSO so you can run the next exercise.

1.2.3 "Hello, World" from TSO

When this is done, you'll see READY. This is the TSO command prompt, similar to C:\> under Windows. It's time for our simplistic, trivial, yet traditional, "Hello, World" example. We'll use the SEND command to send a message with the text "Hello, World" to a user. Think of SEND as TSO's instant messenger (IM). Because the only user that you know right now is yourself, you will be the originator of the message as well as the recipient. Ready (pun intended)? Type this:

```
send 'Hello, World' u(<your user name>)
```

As you can see in Figure 1.6, TSO echoes what you typed. The SEND command processor sends the message to the intended recipient, the user ID ORIPOME. After the SEND command, TSO prompts you with READY to let you know that you can enter more commands.

```
READY
send 'Hello, world' u(oripome)
Hello, world ORIPOME
READY
```

Figure 1.6   "Hello, World" from TSO

Congratulations! You've logged on to TSO and said hello to the world. Note that the only person who saw your exclamation was you, so feel free to experiment with other (business-appropriate, of course!) phrases.

When you are done with the mainframe, you need to log off, using the `logoff` command. If you just close the terminal emulator, the session remains open. If you already closed the terminal emulator and you need to log on while you have a running session, type **s** before the `Reconnect` option, as shown in Figure 1.7.

```
---------------------------- TSO/E LOGON ----------------------------

     Enter LOGON parameters below:              RACF LOGON parameters:

     Userid    ===> ORIPOME

     Password  ===>                             New Password ===>

     Procedure ===> GENERAL                     Group Ident  ===>

     Acct Nmbr ===> ACCT#

     Size      ===>

     Perform   ===>

     Command   ===>

     Enter an 'S' before each option desired below:
            -Nomail          -Nonotice     s -Reconnect      _ -OIDcard
```

Figure 1.7   TSO logon panel with Reconnect

1.3 Job Control Language (JCL)

Entering commands from TSO is one way to accomplish tasks in z/OS, but many other ways exist. One of the most popular and powerful ways is to create files that contain lists of things to do. These lists are called batch jobs and are written in z/OS Job Control Language (JCL), which fulfills roughly the same role as shell scripting languages in UNIX.

1.3.1 Introduction to JCL

JCL is a language with its own unique vocabulary and syntax. Before you can write your first JCL, you need to understand a few z/OS concepts and facilities.

We use JCL to create batch jobs. A batch job is a request that z/OS will execute later. z/OS will choose when to execute the job and how much z/OS resources the job can have based upon the policies that the system administrator has set up. This is a key feature of z/OS: z/OS can manage multiple diverse workloads (jobs) based upon the service level that the installation wants. For example, online financial applications will be given higher priority and, therefore, more z/OS resources, and noncritical work will be given a lower priority and, therefore, fewer z/OS resources. z/OS constantly monitors the resources that are available and how they are consumed, reallocating them to meet the installation goals. We could spend volumes describing just this one feature of z/OS, but this book is supposed to be about security, so we won't.

In your batch job, you will tell z/OS this information:

- You'll give the name of your job, with a `//JOB` statement
- You'll specify the program you want to execute, with a
  `//EXEC PGM=<program name>` statement
- If your program uses or creates any data, you'll point to the data using a `//DD` statement.

Listing 1.1 shows a trivial JCL job. Don't worry about executing this job, or about the exact meaning of each word—we explain them later in this chapter.

Listing 1.1   Trivial Batch Job

```
//MARKNJ JOB CLASS=A,NOTIFY=&SYSUID,MSGCLASS=H
//       EXEC PGM=IEFBR14
```

This job executes an IBM-provided z/OS program called IEFBR14. This is a dummy program that tells z/OS "I'm done and all is well." It requires no input and produces no output other than an indication to the operating system that it completed successfully.

You can also run TSO as a batch job by using JCL to tell z/OS this information:

- The name of the job
- The program to run, which is the TSO interpreter IKJEFT01
- Where to get the input for IKJEFT01 and the commands that you want to execute
- Where to put the output from IKJEFT01, the output from TSO, and the commands that you execute

Listing 1.2 shows a batch job that runs TSO to send a message.

Listing 1.2   Batch Job That Sends a Message Using TSO

```
//TSOJOB   JOB CLASS=A,NOTIFY=&SYSUID,MSGCLASS=H
//         EXEC PGM=IKJEFT01
//SYSTSPRT DD SYSOUT=*
//SYSTSIN  DD *
SEND 'Hello, World' U(ORIPOME)
/*
```

1.3.2 Data Sets

To submit a batch job, you need to understand data sets. As the name implies, a data set is a set or collection of data. Data sets are made up of records. To improve performance, records can be gathered together into blocks. Data sets fill the same function as files and directories in UNIX and Windows.

When you create a data set, you assign it a name. The name can be up to 44 characters long and consists of multiple parts, separated by dots (.). Each part can be up to eight characters. In a RACF-protected system, the first qualifier is either a user ID or a group name. We discuss group names in Chapter 2, "Users and Groups."

Note

This means that in a z/OS system protected by RACF, each data set belongs to either a user or a group. This is different from the situation in UNIX and Linux, where each file has a user and a group. We explain the meaning of data set ownership in Chapter 3, "Protecting Data Sets and Other Resources."

Examples of valid data set names are

- MARKN.BOOK.CNTL
- ORI.LONG$$$.DATASET.NAME.WITHLOTS.OFQUALS
- SYS1.PARMLIB

Examples of data set names that are invalid are

- MARKN.QUALIFIERTOOLONG.CNTL (the middle qualifier is longer than eight characters)
- ORI.THIS.DATA.SET.NAME.IS.WAY.WAY.WAY.TOO.LONG (the total data set name is longer than 44 characters)

The act of creating a data set is called data set allocation. To allocate a data set, you need to tell z/OS a few things about the data set:

- The length of records within the data set expressed in bytes (often called the LRECL)
- The expected size of the data set
- If records are to be blocked, the number of bytes in the block (called the BLKSIZE)
- The organization of the data set (referred to as the DSORG)

Data set organization requires a little explanation. z/OS allows you to define a data set that is partitioned into multiple "mini data sets" called members. This type of data set is called a partitioned data set (PDS). PDSs contain a directory that tells z/OS the name of the member as well as how to locate the member, similar to directories under UNIX, Windows, and Linux. Much of the work that you do in z/OS involves the use of PDS data sets, or their more modern version, the extended PDS called the PDSE or library.

In contrast to UNIX, Linux, and Windows, z/OS requires you to specify the maximum size of each data set, for two reasons. The first is historical—z/OS is backward compatible and can run applications that were developed 40 years ago when disk space was at a premium. The second reason is that z/OS is designed for high-availability applications. When you specify the maximum size of each data set, you can ensure that the important data sets will always have the disk space they need. For simple data sets, such as the ones that we are discussing here, the allocation consists of two parts:

1. The initial size of the data set is called the primary extent. This is the amount of space that z/OS reserves for the data set right now. If you think that your data set might grow in size later, you can specify the size of the secondary extents.

2. If the data set is expected to grow beyond its initial size, additional allocations of disk storage can be given to the data set by specifying the size of the secondary extent. If the primary extent of your data set fills up, z/OS allocates the secondary extent up to 15 times. This allows your data set to grow gradually up to the maximum data set size.

When defining the size of the primary and secondary extents, you can do it in bytes or based on the device geometry in units of space called tracks or cylinders. Understanding these two terms requires understanding how a disk drive works. A disk drive consists of a set of rotating metallic platters upon which data is stored magnetically. Data is written on the disk in sets of concentric circles. Each of these circles is called a track. If you project that track from the top of the stack of platters to the bottom, you have created a cylinder. It is faster to read information that is stored in the same cylinder than information that is spread across cylinders.

1.3.3 Using ISPF to Create and Run Batch Jobs

Before we can create and submit a batch job, we need to create a data set to hold it. The simplest way to allocate a data set is to use the Interactive System Productivity Facility (ISPF).

1.3.3.1 Data Set Creation

Getting into ISPF is very simple: just type ISPF on the TSO command line. ISPF enables you to perform many common z/OS tasks from a full-screen interactive dialog. You move about the ISPF dialogs by specifying the number of the dialog that you want to use. For example, Utilities is option 3. You can then choose the suboption, which enables you to define and delete data sets. That's option 2. We often combine these two and type them as ISPF option 3.2.

As you can see in Figure 1.8, each ISPF panel presents the list of options that you can select. When you get familiar with ISPF, you can use ISPF's fast-path feature and specify =3.2 from any ISPF panel to have ISPF take you directly to the data set allocate and delete panel.

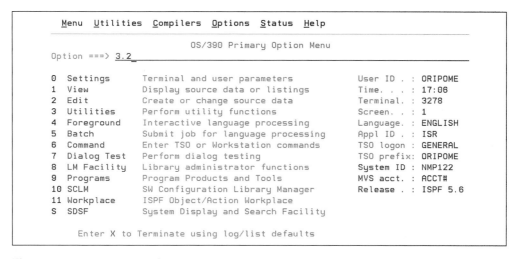

Figure 1.8   Main menu of ISPF

Select option **3.2** and press Enter (or the right Ctrl key). ISPF now takes you to a panel where you can allocate and delete data sets. Type **A** as the option, your user ID as the project (ORIPOME in the screenshot), **RACFBK** as the group, and **CNTL** as the type, as shown in Figure 1.9. By convention, CNTL is used for data sets that store JCL jobs, which correspond roughly to shell scripts or batch files.

```
                            Data Set Utility
      Option ===> a

          A Allocate new data set          C Catalog data set
          R Rename entire data set         U Uncatalog data set
          D Delete entire data set         S Short data set information
     blank Data set information             V VSAM Utilities

      ISPF Library:
         Project  . . ORIPOME        Enter "/" to select option
         Group  . . . RACFBK         /  Confirm Data Set Delete
         Type . . . . CNTL
```

Figure 1.9   Step 1 in data set creation

To allocate the data set, you need to tell z/OS this information:

- The expected size of your data set. We'll be adding other members to this partitioned data set, so let's give it an initial size (primary allocation) of ten tracks and allow it to grow five tracks at a time (secondary allocation). Remember that z/OS uses the secondary allocation 15 times before the data set reaches its maximum size.

- The length of each record in your data set. One of the most common record lengths in z/OS is 80 bytes, which is what we will use for our first few data sets.

- The size of each block. For performance reasons, you might want to tell z/OS that whenever it reads a record, it should read a group of them. That way, when you read the next record, it will already be in memory. Every time z/OS reads from the disk, it reads an entire block. The block size that you select also affects the efficiency of the records stored on the disk drive. If you specify 0, z/OS calculates the best block size for the device upon which the data set is placed.

- The number of directory blocks. When a data set is a partitioned data set, you need to tell z/OS how much space on the data set should be reserved for the directory. Each directory block has enough space to hold the information for about five members. We'll specify 20 blocks, which will give us plenty of space for new members.

- The organization of the data set. Many different types of data sets exist. For our purposes, we'll be working with two types of data sets: normal data sets (called sequential data sets) and partitioned data sets. For this data set, specify PDS for a partitioned data set. Sequential data sets are similar to files under other operating systems. Partitioned data sets contain multiple members, distinguished by name. Each member is similar to a file, so the entire partitioned data set is similar to a directory.

After you have typed all this information, your panel should look similar to Figure 1.10. Press Enter to create the data set. ISPF responds by representing the Data set utility panel with `Data Set Allocated` highlighted in the upper-right corner.

1.3.3.2 Editing Data Set Members

When the data set is created , go to the ISPF editor. To do this, enter **=2** on any command line. This is the ISPF "fast path" to the ISPF edit panel, which is option 2 from the main ISPF menu. On this panel, specify the name of the data set that you just allocated. Because you are editing a PDS, you need to specify either the name of an existing member or the name of a member that you want created, as shown in Figure 1.11. In this example, we're creating a member named HELLOW.

```
                           Allocate New Data Set
        Command ===> _____
                                                          More:       +
        Data Set Name  . . . : ORIPOME.RACFBK.CNTL

        Management class . . . _____    (Blank for default management class)
        Storage class  . . . . _____    (Blank for default storage class)
         Volume serial . . . . _____      (Blank for system default volume) **
         Device type . . . . . _____    (Generic unit or device address) **
        Data class . . . . . . _____    (Blank for default data class)
         Space units . . . . . _____  (BLKS, TRKS, CYLS, KB, MB, BYTES
                                            or RECORDS)
         Average record unit   _           (M, K, or U)
         Primary quantity  . . 10_____  (In above units)
         Secondary quantity    5_____  (In above units)
         Directory blocks  . . 20____      (Zero for sequential data set) *
         Record format . . . . FB____
         Record length . . . . 80____
         Block size  . . . . . 0_____
         Data set name type  : PDS_____    (LIBRARY, HFS, PDS, or blank)  *
```

Figure 1.10   Step 2 in data set creation

```
                            Edit Entry Panel
        Command ===> _____

        ISPF Library:
          Project . . . ORIPOME_
          Group . . . . racfbk_   . . . _____  . . . _____  . . . _____
          Type  . . . . cntl___
          Member  . . . hellow__       (Blank or pattern for member selection list)
```

Figure 1.11   ISPF edit panel

The ISPF Editor

A full description of the ISPF editor with all its features is beyond the scope of this book. For a detailed explanation of the commands, browse to http://publibz.boulder.ibm.com/bookmgr_OS390/libraryserver/zosv1r6/ and open z/OS V1R6.0 Elements, Features, and Software Products → z/OS Elements and Features, z/OS Collection Kit, March 2005 → z/OS V1R6.0 ISPF Edit and Edit Macros → 1.0 Part 1, The ISPF Editor.

After you press Enter, ISPF creates the member and places you in the ISPF editor. At this point, type the JCL shown in Listing 1.2. You need to type it on the lines that start with ''''', under the blue asterisks (*), as shown in Figure 1.12. Remember to change ORIPOME to your own user ID. Traditionally, JCL lines use the eight characters after the // for identifiers or leave them empty when no identifier is required. That is the reason, for example, that the word EXEC on the second line starts on the same column as the word JOB on the first line. The JCL would work with just one space, but it is more readable this way.

```
EDIT        ORIPOME.RACFBK.CNTL(HELLOW) - 01.00              Columns 00001 00072
Command ===> _____       Scroll ===> HALF
xxxxxx ***************************** Top of Data ********************************
==MSG> -Warning- The UNDO command is not available until you change
==MSG>           your edit profile using the command RECOVERY ON.
'''''' //TSOJOB   JOB CLASS=A,NOTIFY=&SYSUID,MSGCLASS=H
'''''' //         EXEC PGM=IKJEFT01
'''''' //SYSTSPRT DD SYSOUT=*
'''''' //SYSTSIN  DD *
'''''' SEND 'Hello, world' U(ORIPOME)
'''''' /*_
''''''
```

Figure 1.12   The editor after typing the batch job

After this is done, press Enter. ISPF saves your changes and replaces the quotes on the left with line numbers.

At this point, you're ready to submit your job. Type **SUBMIT** on the command line, and your batch job is submitted to the job entry subsystem at your installation. You will get a confirmation message with the job number, as shown in Figure 1.13.

```
IKJ56250I JOB TSOJOB(JOB03647) SUBMITTED
*** _
```

Figure 1.13   Job submission confirmation message

Your installation has a policy for executing batch jobs, and that policy determines when your batch job is executed. After it has executed, you can view the output of the job. When your job executes, it sends a message to your TSO user ID. If you are logged on and are accepting messages, the message appears as your batch job executes. If you are not logged on or are not accepting messages, it is saved and displayed when you next log on.

When you see the confirmation message, press Enter again. In all likelihood, your job will have already executed and you will see the message, as well as a job confirmation message, as shown in Figure 1.14.

```
    Hello, world ORIPOME
    00.11.07 JOB03647 $HASP165 TSOJOB   ENDED AT NMS122  MAXCC=0 CN(INTERNAL)
    ***  _
```

Figure 1.14   The message the job sent

When you are done with ISPF, enter **=x** on the command line to tell it to exit. If you get a log data panel, such as the one in Figure 1.15, select option **2** to delete the log. You can then use **LOGOFF** to exit TSO.

```
                             Specify Disposition of Log Data       Member HELLOW saved
        Command ===> _____
                                                                      More:     +
        Log Data Set (ORIPOME.SPFLOG1.LIST) Disposition:
        Process Option . . . . 2  1. Print data set and delete
                                  2. Delete data set without printing
                                  3. Keep data set - Same
                                     (allocate same data set in next session)
                                  4. Keep data set - New
                                     (allocate new data set in next session)
```

Figure 1.15   The log data panel when leaving ISPF

1.3.4 JCL Syntax

Now that you've run the JCL and seen that it works, let's review Listing 1.2 line by line and explain exactly what it does.

First, you'll notice that most lines start with two slashes. The two slashes mark a line as part of JCL. Lines that do not contain those slashes, such as the last two lines in this job, are usually embedded input files.

```
//TSOJOB   JOB CLASS=A,NOTIFY=&SYSUID,MSGCLASS=H
```

This line is the job header. It defines a job called TSOJOB. The CLASS parameter specifies the job's priority, the maximum amount of resources the job is allowed to consume, and so on. A is a good default in most installations, at least for the short jobs we'll use in this book.

The NOTIFY parameter specifies that a user should be notified when the job ends. It could be the name of a user to notify, but here it is &SYSUID, which is a macro that expands to the user who submits the job.

The MSGCLASS parameter specifies that the output of the job needs to be held. This makes it accessible afterward, as you will see in Section 1.3.5, "Viewing the Job Output."

```
//        EXEC PGM=IKJEFT01
```

This line starts an execution step—a step in the batch job that runs a program. It is possible for these steps to be named using an identifier immediately after the two slashes. However, this is a very simple job, so there is no need to identify this stage.

The program that this step executes is IKJEFT01, which is the TSO interpreter.

```
//SYSTSPRT DD SYSOUT=*
```

This line is a data definition. It defines the data stream called SYSTSPRT, which is the output of TSO. SYSOUT=* means that this data stream will go to the standard output of the job. In the next section, you will learn how to get to this output to read it.

```
//SYSTSIN  DD *
```

This line is another data definition. It defines SYSTSIN, which is the input to the TSO interpreter. The value * means that the text that follows is the data to be placed in SYSTSIN.

```
SEND 'Hello, World' U(ORIPOME)
/*
```

This is the input to the TSO interpreter. The first line is a command, the same "Hello, World" command we executed in Section 1.2.3, " 'Hello, World' from TSO." The second line, /*, is a delimiter that means the end of the file.

1.3.5 Viewing the Job Output

One of the outputs from your batch job was the "Hello, World" that was sent to your TSO ID. Your batch job produced other output as well. What happened to that output? It waits in the system until you or your system administrators tell the system what to do with it.

When you submitted the batch job, it was handed over to the job entry subsystem (JES). JES is responsible for scheduling the job, allocating some of its resources, and managing the job's input and output.

IBM provides job entry subsystems: JES2 and JES3. Most of the z/OS environments use JES2, so our examples are oriented toward it. For those of you who are using JES3, equivalent services exist there.

JES2 and JES3

z/OS has two Job Entry Subsystems (JES): JES2 (part of the base z/OS) and JES3 (an optional add-on). Both provide similar capabilities to manage batch jobs and SYSOUT, the job's output data stream. The primary differences are how systems in a SYSPLEX, a mainframe cluster, are managed. In JES2, each system is a peer, selecting work it can process. In JES3, a control system (the global) passes work to other systems (locals) for processing. JES3 also has additional services to provide additional controls over the timing of job execution. Because each JES has its own set of commands and JCL extensions, it is difficult for an installation to change from one JES to another. As a result, mainframe installations generally run the same JES they have used historically.

One of the most popular ways to view the output of your job is to use the IBM System Display and Search Facility (SDSF) program product. You start up SDSF either as a TSO command (SDSF) or as a dialog from within ISPF. In most installations, SDSF is option S from the ISPF Primary Options menu.

From the ISPF Primary Options menu, select the SDSF option, which brings you to the SDSF Primary Option menu, shown in Figure 1.16. On this panel, the options that are presented depend upon your level of authorization: The more things you are authorized to do, the more options you'll see presented by SDSF on the panel.

```
HQX7708 ----------------- SDSF PRIMARY OPTION MENU ------------------------
COMMAND INPUT ===> _                                    SCROLL ===> PAGE

DA    Active users                   INIT  Initiators
I     Input queue                    PR    Printers
O     Output queue                   PUN   Punches
H     Held output queue              RDR   Readers
ST    Status of jobs                 LINE  Lines
                                     NODE  Nodes
LOG   System log                     SO    Spool offload
SR    System requests                SP    Spool volumes
MAS   Members in the MAS
JC    Job classes                    CK    Health checker
SE    Scheduling environments
RES   WLM resources                  ULOG  User session log
ENC   Enclaves
PS    Processes


Licensed Materials - Property of IBM

5694-A01 (C) Copyright IBM Corp. 1981, 2003. All rights reserved.
US Government Users Restricted Rights - Use, duplication or
disclosure restricted by GSA ADP Schedule Contract with IBM Corp.
```

Figure 1.16   The SDSF Primary Option menu

The job's output is in the output queue. Type **o** to enter the output queue, find your job, and type **s** next to it to open the output, as shown in Figure 1.17. If necessary, you can scroll down using F8 or up again using F7.

```
    Display  Filter  View  Print  Options  Help
 ---------------------------------------------------------------------
 SDSF OUTPUT ALL CLASSES ALL FORMS     LINES 531        LINE 1-11 (11)
 COMMAND INPUT ===>                                     SCROLL ===> 1
 NP   JOBNAME  JobID    Owner    Prty C Forms   Dest           Tot-Rec
      SETMSG   STC03613 IBMUSER    9 A STD      LOCAL               31
      IRRDPTAB STC03615 IBMUSER    9 A STD      LOCAL               49
      LOGINT   STC03631 IBMUSER    9 A STD      LOCAL               47
      LOGINT   STC03633 IBMUSER    9 A STD      LOCAL               47
      TSO      STC03635 IBMUSER    9 A STD      LOCAL               21
      FTPD     STC03638 OMVSKERN   9 A STD      LOCAL              149
      BPXAS    STC03628 IBMUSER    9 A STD      LOCAL               35
      BPXAS    STC03630 IBMUSER    9 A STD      LOCAL               35
      BPXAS    STC03627 IBMUSER    9 A STD      LOCAL               35
 S_   TSOJOB   JOB03653 ORIPOME    9 H STD      LOCAL               40
      LOGMSG1  STC03614 IBMUSER    9 X STD      LOCAL               42
```

Figure 1.17   The job's output in the output queue

The top part of the output, shown in Figure 1.18, tells when the job started, when it ended, which user ID was assigned to the job, and other job statistics. JES also displays the JCL. Scroll down a page to see more system-generated messages telling you about the resources allocated for your job. You can scroll up (F7), down (F8), left (F10), and right (F11).

```
SDSF OUTPUT DISPLAY TSOJOB    JOB03655 DSID      2 LINE 0       COLUMNS 02- 81
COMMAND INPUT ===> _                                          SCROLL ===> 1
********************************** TOP OF DATA **********************************
                     J E S 2   J O B   L O G  --  S Y S T E M   I P O 1  --  N O D

21.39.53 JOB03655 ---- THURSDAY,  11 JAN 2007 ----
21.39.53 JOB03655  IRR010I  USERID ORIPOME  IS ASSIGNED TO THIS JOB.
21.39.53 JOB03655  ICH70001I ORIPOME  LAST ACCESS AT 09:38:44 ON THURSDAY, JANUA
21.39.53 JOB03655  $HASP373 TSOJOB    STARTED - INIT A   - CLASS A - SYS IPO1
21.39.53 JOB03655  IEF403I TSOJOB - STARTED - TIME=21.39.53
21.39.53 JOB03655  -                                               --TIMINGS (M
21.39.53 JOB03655  -JOBNAME  STEPNAME PROCSTEP     RC   EXCP   CONN    TCB    SRB
21.39.53 JOB03655  -TSOJOB                         00      8      2    .00    .00
21.39.53 JOB03655  IEF404I TSOJOB - ENDED - TIME=21.39.53
21.39.53 JOB03655  -TSOJOB    ENDED.  NAME-                   TOTAL TCB CPU TIM
21.39.53 JOB03655  $HASP395 TSOJOB    ENDED
------ JES2 JOB STATISTICS ------
  11 JAN 2007 JOB EXECUTION DATE
           6 CARDS READ
          40 SYSOUT PRINT RECORDS
  F1=HELP      F2=SPLIT     F3=END     F4=RETURN    F5=IFIND    F6=BOOK
  F7=UP        F8=DOWN      F9=SWAP    F10=LEFT     F11=RIGHT   F12=RETRIEVE
```

Figure 1.18 The first part of the job's output

The real output of the job is in the last four lines of the job, shown in Figure 1.19. These lines show where we see the batch version of TSO displaying the READY prompt, the echoing of the "Hello, World" command, TSO's READY response, and the generated END statement.

```
READY
SEND 'Hello, world' U(ORIPOME)
READY
END
********************************** BOTTOM OF DATA **********************************
```

Figure 1.19 The output of the job's TSO interpreter

1.3.5.1 Filtering Jobs

A large z/OS installation can have many jobs running at the same time. It is possible to use filtering to see only the jobs that are relevant to you.

To see the current filters, run this command inside SDSF:

```
SET DISPLAY ON
```

To filter, enter the name of the field to filter (prefix in the job name, destination, owner, or sysname) and the value. For example, this command filters for jobs that start with *L*.

```
PREFIX L*
```

After this command, SDSF will show only those jobs that start with *L,* as you can see in Figure 1.20.

```
   SDSF OUTPUT ALL CLASSES ALL FORMS      LINES 139        LINE 1-3 (3)
   COMMAND INPUT ===>  _                                   SCROLL ===>  1
   PREFIX=L*  DEST=(ALL)  OWNER=*  SYSNAME=
   NP   JOBNAME  JobID    Owner    Prty C Forms    Dest             Tot-Rec
        LOGINT   STC03961 IBMUSER     9 A STD      LOCAL                 47
        LOGINT   STC03963 IBMUSER     9 A STD      LOCAL                 50
        LOGMSG1  STC03951 IBMUSER     9 X STD      LOCAL                 42
```

Figure 1.20   Filtered job list in SDSF

To remove the filter, run this command:

```
PREFIX
```

1.4 z/OS UNIX System Services

Many changes have occurred in the world of computing since the announcement of System/360 in 1964. Among the many significant changes is the development of the UNIX operating system by employees at AT&T's Bell Labs in the 1960s. Although UNIX has concepts such as processes and threads, which are analogous to z/OS concepts such as address spaces and tasks, many significant differences exist. For example, in UNIX, files are byte-oriented streams of data, but in z/OS, files (data sets) are record oriented.

Within z/OS, you have a complete UNIX environment with z/OS UNIX System Services. This UNIX environment is integrated with the "traditional" z/OS environment. For example, you can access a z/OS UNIX file from a batch job and you can access a data set from a z/OS UNIX application.

You can enter the world of UNIX from z/OS in several ways. From TSO, you can enter the z/OS UNIX environment using the OMVS command from the TSO READY prompt. Within the ISPF environment, you can type the command **tso omvs** to enter UNIX (in general, you can run any TSO command from ISPF by prefacing it with tso).

Why OMVS?

When IBM first added the UNIX environment to MVS, it was called Open Edition, with the "Open" designating this environment and set of interfaces as one that was not designed or owned by IBM. The logical extension of this is Open MVS, which was shortened to the command OMVS. You can see vestiges of this naming convention in the OMVS command, the OMVS segment in user profiles, and the z/OS UNIX "O" commands, such as OGET, OPUT, and OEDIT.

Regardless of the way you enter it, OMVS provides a shell interface where you can type UNIX commands, as shown in Figure 1.21. By default, you type commands close to the bottom, at the ===> prompt (it is possible to configure OMVS to place the ===> prompt at the top instead).

```
IBM
Licensed Material - Property of IBM
5694-A01 (C) Copyright IBM Corp. 1993, 2004
 (C) Copyright Mortice Kern Systems, Inc., 1985, 1996.
 (C) Copyright Software Development Group, University of Waterloo, 1989.

All Rights Reserved.

U.S. Government users - RESTRICTED RIGHTS - Use, Duplication, or
Disclosure restricted by GSA-ADP schedule contract with IBM Corp.

IBM is a registered trademark of the IBM Corp.

ORIPOME:/u/oripome #>echo Hello, world
Hello, world
ORIPOME:/u/oripome #>




  ===> echo this is where you type commands _
                                                                   INPUT
```

Figure 1.21   OMVS shell

Can we do our "Hello, World" example as a z/OS UNIX program? Sure! Let's do it in the C programming language. Start by using OEDIT, which is the ISPF editor for z/OS UNIX:

```
oedit test.c
```

You are now in an editor that is very similar to the editor that you used to edit your JCL. This time, enter the "Hello, World" program, as shown in Figure 1.22. When you are done, press **F3** to exit the editor. If it asks about log file disposition, as in Figure 1.15, enter **2** to delete it.

```
EDIT        /u/oripome/test.c                          Columns 00001 00072
Command ===>                                           Scroll ===> HALF
****** ***************************** Top of Data *****************************
==MSG> -Warning- The UNDO command is not available until you change
==MSG>           your edit profile using the command RECOVERY ON.
''''''  #include <stdio.h>
......
''''''  main ()
......  {
''''''      printf("Hello, world\n");
''''''  }_
......
```

Figure 1.22   "Hello, World" program in C for OMVS

Now compile and execute the program:

```
c89 -o test test.c
./test
```

It should write the message, as shown in Figure 1.23. If the compiler fails, type **exit** from OMVS and **LOGOFF** from TSO. Then when you log back on, type **2096128** in the size field of the TSO logon panel, the panel shown in Figure 1.7 earlier. Note that the C compiler is a separate product from OMVS, and your site might not have it.

The TSO Size Field

The size field in the TSO logon screen specifies the region size, the maximum amount of memory that will be allocated to you for that TSO logon. The C compiler requires a lot of memory, so you might need to increase this number from the default to about 2MB.

In JCL jobs, you can use REGION=<number> to specify the same information.

```
ORIPOME:/u/oripome #>oedit test.c
ORIPOME:/u/oripome #>c89 -o test test.c
ORIPOME:/u/oripome #>./test
Hello, world
ORIPOME:/u/oripome #>
```

Figure 1.23   Execution of the "Hello, World" program in C for OMVS

When you are done with OMVS, use **exit** to leave it.

1.5 Getting Help

At this point, we would like to write that you are completely comfortable with the mainframe's user interface and that you know how to do everything you might need to learn RACF. However, that would be a bold-faced lie. We could have filled the entire book with directions on how to use the mainframe and still not included everything you might need.

Instead, this section teaches you how to get help when you need it.

1.5.1 Context-Sensitive Help

The mainframe itself has a lot of documentation for your use.

1.5.1.1 TSO

To get help on a TSO command, type **HELP <name of command>**. For example, Figure 1.24 shows the help text for the ISPF command. The prompt at the bottom (***) shows that more information is available if you press Enter.

```
    READY
  help ispf

  FUNCTION -
    THE ISPF COMMAND IS USED TO START THE ISPF PROGRAM DEVELOPMENT
    FACILITY (PDF).  PDF CAN BE INVOKED SPECIFYING EITHER THE "PANEL",
    "CMD", OR "PGM" KEYWORDS.  IF NEITHER "PANEL", "CMD", OR "PGM" IS
    SPECIFIED, THE "ISR@PRIM" PRIMARY OPTION PANEL IS DISPLAYED.  FOR
    MORE INFORMATION ABOUT THIS FACILITY, ENTER THE "ISPF" COMMAND,
    THEN SELECT THE "TUTORIAL" OPTION AS DIRECTED ON THE DISPLAY.


  SYNTAX -
        ISPF    OPTION
                 OR
               PANEL('NAME')   OPT('OPT')
                 OR
               CMD('COMMAND')   LANG(APL|CREX)
                 OR
               PGM('NAME')   PARM('PARM')

               NEWAPPL('APPLID')
  ***  _
```

Figure 1.24   Output of the TSO HELP command

This help file shows that you can run ISPF with an option to immediately reach whatever panel you need. Use this to get to the ISPF data set utility panel, which is option 3 from the main menu followed by option 2 from the Utilities menu.

```
ISPF 3.2
```

1.5.1.2 ISPF

Inside ISPF, you can press F1 for context-sensitive help. For example, Figure 1.25 shows the context-sensitive help for the data set utilities panel. Inside the help panel, you can press **Enter** to advance to the next screen, or choose an option from the menu (if available). To get back to the panel, press **F3**.

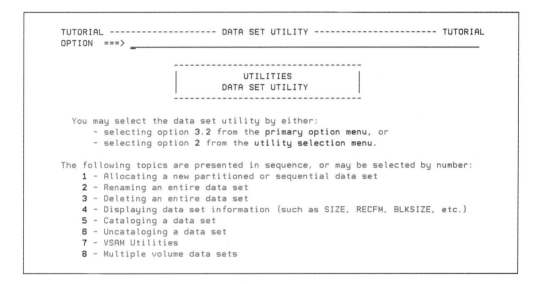

```
TUTORIAL -------------------- DATA SET UTILITY ----------------------- TUTORIAL
OPTION  ===> _____

                    -------------------------------------
                   |              UTILITIES              |
                   |           DATA SET UTILITY          |
                    -------------------------------------

    You may select the data set utility by either:
        - selecting option 3.2 from the primary option menu, or
        - selecting option 2 from the utility selection menu.

    The following topics are presented in sequence, or may be selected by number:
        1 - Allocating a new partitioned or sequential data set
        2 - Renaming an entire data set
        3 - Deleting an entire data set
        4 - Displaying data set information (such as SIZE, RECFM, BLKSIZE, etc.)
        5 - Cataloging a data set
        6 - Uncataloging a data set
        7 - VSAM Utilities
        8 - Multiple volume data sets
```

Figure 1.25   ISPF context-sensitive help for the data set utilities panel

1.5.1.3 OMVS

In OMVS, you can press **F1** to get help about the shell itself. To get help for a specific command, use man <name of command>, as you would in any other version of UNIX.

1.5.2. The Manuals

IBM makes the manuals for z/OS available at http://publibz.boulder.ibm.com/bookmgr_OS390/
libraryserver. Select your z/OS version and you will see a list of manuals, as shown in Figure 1.26.

For example, Figure 1.27 shows part of *z/OS 1R5.0-1R6.0 TSO/E User's Guide*, Topic
1.1.2.1, "Issuing the LOGON Command." This manual, similar to most manuals we will use in this
book, is available under z/OS Elements and Features—z/OS Collection Kit (the top subdirectory
in the list of manuals).

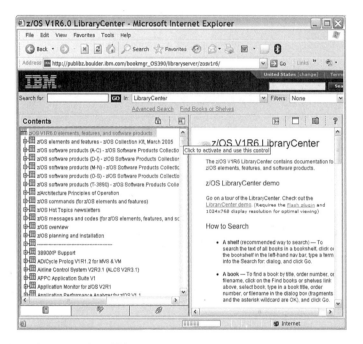

Figure 1.26   List of manuals for z/OS 1.6

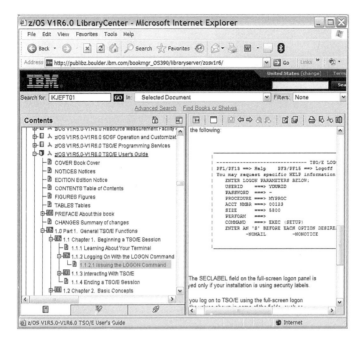

Figure 1.27   Example of a topic in a z/OS manual

1.6 Additional Information

A plethora of additional information is available on mainframes. Some of our favorite references are

- The IBM Redbooks® web site. Redbooks are books written by technical professionals working with the IBM International Technical Support Organization (ITSO). These books (and shorter works called Redpieces) are tactical "how to" books on a variety of subjects. The books and Redpieces "Introduction to the New Mainframe: z/OS Basics" and "Introduction to the New Mainframe: Networking" are available for free from the IBM Redbooks web site at www.redbooks.ibm.com. We highly recommend the books *Introduction to the New Mainframe: z/OS Basics*, *Introduction to the New Mainframe: Networking*, *Introduction to the New Mainframe: Security*, and *C/C++ Applications on z/OS and OS/390 UNIX*.

- The IBM publications web site for z/OS at www.ibm.com/servers/eserver/zseries/zos/bkserv/. From this web site, you can find almost all the product publications for the various z/OS products.

- z/OS ISPF Edit and Edit Macros, which explains the ISPF editor. It is available on the IBM publication web site for z/OS.

- *IBM's 360 and Early 370 Systems,* by Emerson W. Pugh, Lyle R. Johnson, and John H. Palmer (MIT Press, 1991), the definitive history of the development of the System/360.

- The IBM Archives, which contain a wealth of history of the mainframe, at www.ibm. com/ibm/history/exhibits/mainframe/mainframe_intro.html.

CHAPTER 2

Users and Groups

In this chapter, you learn how to create users and groups using RACF.

2.1 Creating a User

The easiest way to control RACF is from the ISPF menus. Select `Programs` from the main ISPF menu. A list of applications is displayed, one of which is RACF. Enter the appropriate number to select RACF. In this installation, the application number happens to be 1, as shown in Figure 2.1. If numerous applications are shown, you might need to scroll down by pressing F8 to locate the RACF application. You can press F7 to scroll back up.

```
                       z/OS Application Menu
       Option ===> 1_
                                           More:       +
       1  RACF           OS/390 Security Server
       2  SMP/E          SMP/E Installed with z/OS
       3  OE Browse      OpenEdition Browse Files
       4  OE Edit        OpenEdition Edit Files
       5  ISPF Shell     OpenMVS ISPF Shell
```

Figure 2.1   RACF in the ISPF programs menu

This selection takes you to the main RACF menu, shown in Figure 2.2. Select **4** for user-related options.

```
                                RACF - SERVICES OPTION MENU
     OPTION ===> 4_

     SELECT ONE OF THE FOLLOWING:

        1  DATA SET PROFILES

        2  GENERAL RESOURCE PROFILES

        3  GROUP PROFILES AND USER-TO-GROUP CONNECTIONS

        4  USER PROFILES AND YOUR OWN PASSWORD

        5  SYSTEM OPTIONS

        6  REMOTE SHARING FACILITY

        7  DIGITAL CERTIFICATES AND KEY RINGS
       99  EXIT
```

Figure 2.2   The RACF main menu

To add a user, select option **1** and enter the name of the user in the USER field, as shown in Figure 2.3.

```
                                RACF - USER PROFILE SERVICES
     OPTION ===> 1

     SELECT ONE OF THE FOLLOWING:

              1    ADD         Add a user profile
              2    CHANGE      Change a user profile
              3    DELETE      Delete a user profile
              4    PASSWORD    Change your own password or interval
              5    AUDIT       Monitor user activity (Auditors only)


        D or 8   DISPLAY     Display profile contents
        S or 9   SEARCH      Search the RACF data base for profiles


     ENTER THE FOLLOWING INFORMATION:

        USER     ===> myuser_     Userid
```

Figure 2.3   First step in user creation

Next, you must add information for the user who was just created. Enter a name for the user and type the password twice, as shown in Figure 2.4. Enter your own user ID as the owner. The owner is any user or group authorized to manage a RACF entity. In this example, the RACF entity you are managing is the user MYUSER.

```
                          RACF - ADD USER MYUSER
    COMMAND ===>

    ENTER THE FOLLOWING INFORMATION:

       OWNER                    ===> ORIPOME      Userid or group name

       USER NAME                ===> Sample User

       DEFAULT GROUP            ===>              Group name

       PASSWORD                 ===>              User's initial password
                                ===>        _     Re-enter password to verify
```

Figure 2.4   Second step in user creation

This creates a user account. Because RACF serves as the user registry for z/OS, the user-specific information that is required for systems such as TSO and UNIX System Services is also specified from RACF. To configure additional user information for this account, enter **YES** in the optional information field, as shown in Figure 2.5.

```
                          RACF - ADD USER MYUSER
    COMMAND ===>

    TO ASSIGN USER ATTRIBUTES, ENTER YES:

       GROUP ACCESS    ===> NO           SPECIAL       ===> NO
       ADSP            ===> NO           OPERATIONS    ===> NO
       OIDCARD         ===> NO           AUDITOR       ===> NO
       NO-PASSWORD     ===> NO           RESTRICTED    ===> NO

    IDENTIFY THE MODEL PROFILE FOR USER DATA SETS (OPTIONAL):

       MODEL PROFILE    ===>

    TO CREATE THE FOLLOWING, ENTER YES (OPTIONAL):

       A GENERIC DATA SET PROFILE        ===> NO
       A MINIDISK PROFILE                ===> NO


    TO ADD OPTIONAL INFORMATION, ENTER YES    ===> yes _
```

Figure 2.5   Enter optional information for the new user.

This user needs to use TSO. To configure TSO access for MYUSER, enter ? next to TSO PARAMETERS and press Enter, as shown in Figure 2.6.

```
                          RACF - ADD USER MYUSER
    COMMAND ===>

    To ADD the following information, enter any character:

        _ CLASS AUTHORITY                 _ NDS PARAMETERS
        _ INSTALLATION DATA               _ KERB PARAMETERS
        _ GROUP AUTHORITY                 _ LDAP PROXY PARAMETERS
        _ SECURITY LEVEL or CATEGORIES    _ ENTERPRISE IDENTITY MAPPING
        _ SECURITY LABEL
        _ LOGON RESTRICTIONS
        _ NATIONAL LANGUAGES
        _ DFP PARAMETERS
        ? TSO PARAMETERS
        _ OPERPARM PARAMETERS
        _ CICS PARAMETERS
        _ WORK ATTRIBUTES
        _ OMVS PARAMETERS
```

Figure 2.6   Selecting TSO parameters

This user will start ISPF automatically at logon. To configure this, set LOGON PROCEDURE NAME to GENERAL or to a different value used for general-purpose users in your installation (ask a system programmer). Set COMMAND to ISPF. The COMMAND setting is similar to the logon shell in UNIX in the /etc/passwd file. Figure 2.7 shows the completed panel.

```
                          RACF - ADD USER MYUSER
                          TSO-RELATED INFORMATION
    COMMAND ===>


    ENTER THE FOLLOWING TSO-RELATED INFORMATION:

        JOB CLASS             ===>
        MESSAGE CLASS         ===>
        HOLD CLASS            ===>
        SYSOUT CLASS          ===>
        ACCOUNT NUMBER        ===>
        LOGON PROCEDURE NAME  ===> general
        REGION SIZE           ===>
        UNIT                  ===>
        DESTINATION ID        ===>
        MAXIMUM REGION SIZE   ===>
        USER DATA             ===>
        LOGON SECURITY LABEL  ===>
        COMMAND               ===> ispf_
                              ===>
```

Figure 2.7   TSO parameters to start ISPF automatically

Log on as MYUSER on a separate terminal emulation window. At this initial login, the new user will be required to enter a new password. Because you set COMMAND to ISPF earlier, MYUSER will enter ISPF automatically upon logging in.

Note that MYUSER enters ISPF automatically, but it is still a TSO logon. At the end of the session, MYUSER must exit ISPF first with =x, and then must exit TSO with logoff.

2.2 How to Modify a User for OMVS Access

At this point, MYUSER can log on to TSO and ISPF. However, MYUSER cannot log on to OMVS, which will be needed later. This section shows you how to give the user the ability to access OMVS.

2.2.1 Modifying the User

Return to the RACF user profiles menu, shown in Figure 2.3, type the user name, and select option **2** to change the user.

No changes are required in the first page, so press Enter.

On the second page, enter **yes** to add or change optional information, as shown in Figure 2.8.

```
                         RACF - CHANGE USER MYUSER
     COMMAND ===>

     TO ASSIGN A USER ATTRIBUTE, ENTER YES
     TO CANCEL A USER ATTRIBUTE, ENTER NO

        GROUP ACCESS        ===>              SPECIAL        ===>
        ADSP                ===>              OPERATIONS     ===>
        OIDCARD             ===>              AUDITOR        ===>
        NO-PASSWORD         ===>              RESTRICTED     ===>

     CHANGE OR DELETE THE MODEL PROFILE USED FOR USER DATA SETS (OPTIONAL):

        NEW MODEL           ===>
        DELETE              ===>              YES if no model is to be used


     TO ADD OR CHANGE OPTIONAL INFORMATION, ENTER YES     ===> yes _
```

Figure 2.8   Selecting to modify optional information

To enable OMVS access for MYUSER, type a character next to OMVS PARAMETERS and press Enter, as shown in Figure 2.9.

> **Note**
>
> On many RACF panels, you can just type any character instead of the underline (_) to select an option. Figure 2.9 shows a question mark used for this. Figure 2.10 shows the letters x, q, and r.

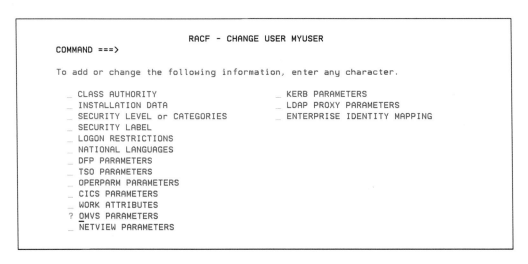

```
                         RACF - CHANGE USER MYUSER
 COMMAND ===>

 To add or change the following information, enter any character.

    _ CLASS AUTHORITY                    _ KERB PARAMETERS
    _ INSTALLATION DATA                  _ LDAP PROXY PARAMETERS
    _ SECURITY LEVEL or CATEGORIES       _ ENTERPRISE IDENTITY MAPPING
    _ SECURITY LABEL
    _ LOGON RESTRICTIONS
    _ NATIONAL LANGUAGES
    _ DFP PARAMETERS
    _ TSO PARAMETERS
    _ OPERPARM PARAMETERS
    _ CICS PARAMETERS
    _ WORK ATTRIBUTES
    ? OMVS PARAMETERS
    _ NETVIEW PARAMETERS
```

Figure 2.9   Choosing to change OMVS parameters

Provide the required parameters for the UID, HOME, and PROGRAM fields. You can select the HOME and PROGRAM parameters using any character. For the UID to be assigned automatically, select the AUTOUID option. This is shown in Figure 2.10.

Enter **/u/myuser** as the value for the home directory, as shown in Figure 2.11. Note that all the lines beginning with => comprise a continuous RACF input field. This is a RACF generic input field element.

```
                            RACF - CHANGE USER TESTUSR
                               OMVS PARAMETERS
        COMMAND ===>

        Delete ALL OMVS information      (NOOMVS)  ____    Enter YES to DELETE

           -- OR --

        Choose to CHANGE or DELETE, then press ENTER.
                                                              More:     +
        Specify new User Identifier       (UID)  _____  0 - 2147483647
        Allow shared use of this UID     (SHARED)  _          Enter any character
           -- or --
        Assign a unique UID              (AUTOUID)  x          Enter any character
           -- or --
        Delete User Identifier            (NOUID)  _          Enter any character

        Change Initial Path Name          (HOME)  q           Enter any character
        Delete Initial Path Name         (NOHOME)  _          Enter any character

        Change Program Path Name         (PROGRAM)  r _       Enter any character
        Delete Program Path Name        (NOPROGRAM)  _        Enter any character
```

Figure 2.10 OMVS parameters

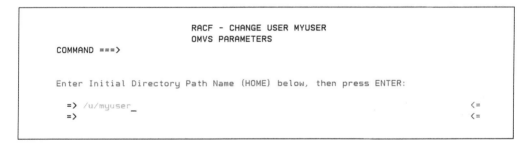

```
                            RACF - CHANGE USER MYUSER
                               OMVS PARAMETERS
        COMMAND ===>


        Enter Initial Directory Path Name (HOME) below, then press ENTER:

          => /u/myuser_                                              <=
          =>                                                         <=
```

Figure 2.11 Entering the home directory

Set the shell program path name to **/bin/sh**, as shown in Figure 2.12.

```
                         RACF - CHANGE USER MYUSER
                         OMVS PARAMETERS
   COMMAND ===>


   Enter Program Path Name (PROGRAM), then press ENTER:

     => /bin/sh                                                    <=
     => _                                                          <=
```

Figure 2.12   Entering the shell

At this point, MYUSER will be able to use UNIX System Services. For example, MYUSER will be able to enter OMVS from TSO.

On some systems, creating a user with AUTOUID fails, as shown in Figure 2.13.

```
   IRR52183I Use of automatic UID assignment requires SHARED.IDS to be implemented

   ***
```

Figure 2.13   AUTOUID failure

In such a case, you must determine an unused UID manually. In this case, ask a local system programmer what is the procedure in your site.

2.2.2 Creating the OMVS Home Directory (and Modifying Users from TSO)

To be productive, MYUSER must be provided a home directory to use OMVS. Your user might not be authorized to create /u/myuser. To create that directory, you must have permission to write to /u. You can do that in several ways, but the easiest at this point is for you to change your UID to 0 to become root.

> ### Warning
>
> This is not the proper way to do this; you should get specific authorization instead. However, the next chapter explains authorizations, and we wanted you to be able to see MYUSER using OMVS now.
>
> What you are about to do here violates security procedures on almost all production systems. We suggest this method only if you are *not* on a production system. On a production system, you must ask the service owner for OMVS what to do.

You already know how to modify a user from ISPF, so now you will do it from the TSO command line. The RACF command-line interface is documented in Chapter 5, "RACF Command Syntax," of *z/OS V1R6.0 Security Server RACF Command Language Reference* (or the equivalent for other versions of z/OS). If you do not remember how to get to it, refer back to Section 1.5.2, "The Manuals."

First, run this command to get your current UID from the OMVS READY prompt:

```
LISTUSER <your user name> OMVS
```

This command shows your general RACF user profile and then the OMVS section with the UID, as shown in Figure 2.14. It is somewhat similar to the id command under UNIX that shows user information, except that the information shown is much more extensive. You might need to press Enter to allow it to scroll some of the information. Make a note of this UID; you will need it later.

```
OMVS INFORMATION
----------------
UID= 0000000100
HOME= /u/oripome
CPUTIMEMAX= NONE
ASSIZEMAX= NONE
FILEPROCMAX= NONE
PROCUSERMAX= NONE
THREADSMAX= NONE
MMAPAREAMAX= NONE
```

Figure 2.14   LISTUSER OMVS output

Next, run this command to change your OMVS UID to zero. Notice the syntax: OMVS followed by all the OMVS parameters in parenthesis. The only OMVS parameter is UID, which is again followed by the value, 0, in parenthesis. This command is roughly equivalent to editing /etc/passwd to change user information.

> **Note**
>
> As explained earlier, this is *not* how you should do things in a production environment. We are using this method here for expedience, with the assumption that you are running on a test system where you have administrator privileges in RACF. On a production system, special permissions can be specified to control precisely who can perform operations such as creating a new user's home directory. You will learn about these later in this book. For now, we are using this method only to get you up and running quickly.

```
ALTUSER <your user name> OMVS(UID(0))
```

Now you can repeat the `LISTUSER` command to see that your UID is zero. OMVS is a version of UNIX, so UID zero is interpreted as the super user. Now you can enter OMVS again and run the following command to create a home directory for MYUSER:

```
mkdir /u/myuser
chown myuser /u/myuser
```

The final step is to return your UID to its original value. Run this command:

```
ALTUSER <your user name> OMVS(UID(<your original UID>))
```

2.2.3 Verifying MYUSER Has OMVS Access

You are finally ready to log on as MYUSER and enter OMVS. Because you are running inside ISPF, you must enter this command:

```
TSO OMVS
```

Note

This is the way to get to OMVS from ISPF. You can also run OMVS from the TSO command line or use Telnet.

2.3 Groups

When the number of users is relatively small, you could manage them directly. However, mainframes are usually used in large environments with many users. RACF supports user groups to simplify the administration of a large number of users.

A user can belong to multiple groups, in which case the user's permissions are the union of the permissions provided by all the groups to which the user belongs (to which the user is connected, in mainframe terminology).

Groups can own other groups, resulting in a hierarchy. Note, however, that this hierarchy is only for group-management purposes. Users get permissions from the groups to which they are connected, but not from permissions of groups higher in the hierarchy. If group EARTH contains groups US and BRITAIN, and group US is connected to user ORIPOME, that user will have permissions from US but not from EARTH. Exceptions to this rule exist, but they are complex and beyond the scope of an introductory book.

This section teaches you how to search groups and display group information, which is similar to the way you search and display users. Also, the way to create and modify groups is similar to the way to create and modify users, which you learned earlier in this chapter.

2.3.1 Searching Groups

The next chapter covers how to assign permissions to users and groups. To begin learning about groups, we examine the existing ones. Begin by navigating to the main RACF Services Options menu and enter option **3** for group management. In the group menu, shown in Figure 2.15, enter **s** to get a list of RACF groups.

```
                         RACF - GROUP PROFILE SERVICES
        OPTION ===>  s_

          SELECT ONE OF THE FOLLOWING.

                 1  ADD            Add a group profile
                 2  CHANGE         Change a group profile
                 3  DELETE         Delete a group profile
                 4  CONNECT        Add or change a user connection
                 5  REMOVE         Remove users from the group


            D or 8  DISPLAY        Display profile contents
            S or 9  SEARCH         Search the RACF data base for profiles


        ENTER THE FOLLOWING INFORMATION.

           GROUP NAME       ===>
```

Figure 2.15   Group management menu

Figure 2.16 shows the group search panel. In this panel, you can specify the criteria for displayed groups. If you do not specify any criteria, as in the figure, you get all the groups defined in RACF.

```
                         RACF - SEARCH FOR GROUP PROFILES
        COMMAND ===>

        ENTER OPTIONAL SELECTION CRITERIA:
                                                            More:      +

           MASK1    _            Selects group profiles with names that begin
                                 with the specified character string.

           MASK2    _____     Selects group profiles with names that contain
                                 the specified string somewhere after MASK1.

           FILTER   _____     Input filter string.

           AGE      ____         Selects group profiles created before the
                                 number of days specified.

           USERID   _____     Selects the group profiles of which the
                                 specified user is a member.

           GID      _____     Selects profiles which have this GID defined in the
                                 OMVS segment (other options will be ignored).
```

Figure 2.16   Group search panel

Pressing Enter retrieves the list of groups, as shown in Figure 2.17. Choose a group name to use later and then press F3 to close the list.

```
    BROWSE - RACF COMMAND OUTPUT---------------------- LINE 00000000 COL 001 080
    COMMAND ===> _                                        SCROLL ===> PAGE
    ********************************* Top of Data **********************************
    BIBLIO
    CBADMGP
    CBASR1
    CBASR2
    CBCFG1
    CBCLGP
```

Figure 2.17   Group search results

2.3.2 Displaying a Group

To display group information, type **D** as the option and enter the group name. Figure 2.18 uses the group name DB2PM.

```
                        RACF - GROUP PROFILE SERVICES          PROFILE(S) FOUND
    OPTION ===> d_

      SELECT ONE OF THE FOLLOWING.

            1   ADD           Add a group profile
            2   CHANGE        Change a group profile
            3   DELETE        Delete a group profile
            4   CONNECT       Add or change a user connection
            5   REMOVE        Remove users from the group


      D or 8  DISPLAY         Display profile contents
      S or 9  SEARCH          Search the RACF data base for profiles


    ENTER THE FOLLOWING INFORMATION.

      GROUP NAME      ===> DB2PM
```

Figure 2.18   Displaying group information

You can select to display additional group information in the next panel, shown in Figure 2.19. This is useful for groups that affect additional products, such as those that correspond to a UNIX group in UNIX System Services.

```
                        RACF - DISPLAY FOR GROUP PROFILE
  COMMAND ===>

  To select the following options, enter any character.


    _   Include DFP information

  x _Include OMVS information

    _   Include OVM information

    _   Exclude basic RACF information
```

Figure 2.19   Panel for selecting additional group information

Figure 2.20 shows the top part of the group information. It shows the superior group, the group to which this group belongs, as well as all the subgroups and users that this group contains. Users are shown with their permission levels, as explained in Section 2.3.3, "Connecting Users to a Group."

```
    BROWSE - RACF COMMAND OUTPUT----------------------- LINE 00000000 COL 001 080
    COMMAND ===> _                                        SCROLL ===> PAGE
    ******************************** Top of Data ************************************
  INFORMATION FOR GROUP DB2PM
      SUPERIOR GROUP=SYS1         OWNER=THACKER
      NO INSTALLATION DATA
      NO MODEL DATA SET
      TERMUACC
      NO SUBGROUPS
      USER(S)=     ACCESS=     ACCESS COUNT=     UNIVERSAL ACCESS=
        SYSADM       USE          000000               NONE
          CONNECT ATTRIBUTES=NONE
          REVOKE DATE=NONE                   RESUME DATE=NONE
        USER1        USE          000000               NONE
          CONNECT ATTRIBUTES=NONE
          REVOKE DATE=NONE                   RESUME DATE=NONE

  NO OMVS INFORMATION
    ******************************** Bottom of Data *********************************
```

Figure 2.20   Group information

2.3.3 Connecting Users to a Group

To make a user a member of a group, the user is "connected" to that group. To connect users to a group, go to the group profile services panel, shown in Figure 2.15. Enter the group name and select option **4**. In Figure 2.21, we are adding MYUSER to the OMVS group. Enter **myuser** as the user, enter **none** as the default UACC, specify the default access level, and enter **use** as the group authority.

```
                        RACF - ADD OR CHANGE CONNECTION TO OMVS
         COMMAND ===>

         IDENTIFY THE USER:

            USER                    ===> myuser      Userid

         ENTER THE CONNECTION INFORMATION TO BE ADDED OR CHANGED:

            OWNER                   ===> ORIPOME      Userid or group name


            DEFAULT UACC            ===> none         NONE, READ, UPDATE,
                                                      CONTROL, or ALTER

            GROUP AUTHORITY         ===> use          USE, CREATE, CONNECT,
                                                      or JOIN

                        Press ENTER to continue.
```

Figure 2.21   Panel to connect a user to a group

The default Universal Access Authority (UACC) field determines the level of permissions for resources such as data sets that the user will create while connected to the group. In almost all cases, it is better to use a default permission level of None and then give users the permissions they require using data-set specific ACLs, as you will learn in the next chapter.

The Principle of Least Privilege

This suggestion is based on the Principle of Least Privilege, which states that users should be given the minimum level of permissions to accomplish their jobs. With not enough permission, someone might encounter a problem in doing his or her job. As a security administrator, you will be informed about this and can correct the problem. If given too much permission, no user is likely to complain immediately. The problem becomes apparent only when a security audit or break-in occurs, or when someone loses vital data in a file because someone accessed the data inappropriately.

Four levels of group authority affect a user's ability to access and modify group resources:

- **Use**—Use the resources of the group. A user with this level can access the shared resources of the group. For example, a user with this level might be able to read a group data set, a data set that belongs to the group (depending on the ACL).

- **Create**—Adds the right to create new data sets that members of this group can access. Typically, you give this permission level to someone in the group who is responsible for configuring new applications.
- **Connect**—Adds the right to add existing users to the group. This might be given to a manager or team lead who needs to add existing users to the group when their job role requires access.
- **Join**—Adds the right to create new users (who will be members of the group), the right to add new subgroups, and the right to change users' permission level on the group. This might be a Human Resources person who needs to be able to define new users.

Separation of Duties

The separation of duties principle states that when an operation is particularly sensitive or tempting, it should require more than one person. The temptation to commit fraud is significantly less when it requires a conspiracy of several people.

You can use the different levels of permissions to implement separation of duties for account creation. Give one person join permissions on a group that has no resources, and the other connect permission on the group with the resources. The first person has to create the RACF user, and the second person has to connect the user to the group.

Keep the default options on the next panel, shown in Figure 2.22. To review their meanings, click F1 to see context-sensitive help. The bottom three options, SPECIAL, OPERATIONS, and AUDITOR, enable you to define a user as a group administrator. Chapter 6, "Limited-Authority RACF Administrators," explains this in detail.

```
                    RACF - ADD OR CHANGE CONNECTION TO OMVS
    COMMAND ===>

  TO ALLOW USER ATTRIBUTES, ENTER YES
  TO DENY  USER ATTRIBUTES, ENTER NO

    GROUP ACCESS        ===>  _          Allow the group to access new group
                                         data sets

    ADSP                ===>             Create discrete profiles for new
                                         permanent data sets

    REVOKE              ===>             YES, mm/dd/yy (date), or blank

    RESUME              ===>             YES, mm/dd/yy (date), or blank

    SPECIAL             ===>             Grant group-SPECIAL attribute

    OPERATIONS          ===>             Grant group-OPERATIONS attribute

    AUDITOR             ===>             Grant group-AUDITOR attribute
```

Figure 2.22   User-group connection attributes

You can now repeat the procedure in Section 2.3.2, "Displaying a Group," to verify that MYUSER was added to OMVS correctly. This concludes the exercises for this chapter. By this point, you should be able to create and modify users and groups.

2.4 zSecure

IBM Tivoli zSecure is an optional IBM product that simplifies RACF administration. Full description of zSecure is beyond the scope of this book, but we can show you how to do basic RACF operations with it.

To create a new user, start the zSecure shell (xc2r) and run **RA.U** to edit RACF users. Then select Add New User or Segment. In the new user screen, enter the user name, the default group, the password, the owner, and which segments of the user profile will be needed, as shown in Figure 2.23.

```
   Menu    Options   Info    Commands    Setup
                         zSecure Admin+Audit for RACF - RACF - User Add
   Command ===>

   Userid  . . . . . .  MYUSER    (required)
   Default group . . .  CR540    (required for new userid)
   Password  . . . . .          . . .        (twice, required for new userid)
   Owned by  . . . . .  ORIPOME  (may also be set in the follow on update dialog)
   Password phrase . .
                                             (14-100 chars, in single quotes)

   /   Define new userid

   _   Add CICS segment            _   Add NETVIEW segment
   _   Add DCE segment             /   Add OMVS segment
   _   Add DFP segment             _   Add OPERPARM segment
   _   Add EIM segment             _   Add OVM segment
   _   Add KERB segment            _   Add PROXY segment
   _   Add LANGUAGE segment        /   Add TSO segment
   _   Add LNOTES segment          _   Add WORKATTR segment
   _   Add NDS segment
```

Figure 2.23   zSecure new user panel

Then, in the segments list, select the segments you want to see and modify using **s**, as shown in Figure 2.24.

```
   zSecure Admin+Audit for RACF Display Selection          .        Line 1 of 3
   Command ===>                                              Scroll===> PAGE

     Name     Summary Records Title
   _ BASE          1        1 zSecure Admin+Audit for RACF USER MYUSER overview
   s OMVS          1        1 zSecure Admin+Audit for RACF USER MYUSER OMVS segmen
   s TSO           1        1 zSecure Admin+Audit for RACF USER MYUSER TSO segment
   ****************************** Bottom of Data ********************************
```

Figure 2.24   zSecure user segments

You get a screen for each segment you selected. On each screen, you enter the information for that segment, as shown in Figure 2.25 for the OMVS segment.

Groups are manipulated the same way, using RA.G.

```
zSecure Admin+Audit for RACF USER MYUSER OMVS segments          Line 1 of 17
Command ===> _____        Scroll===> PAGE
Users like MYUSER                                 19 Jun 2007 21:38


    Identification                                                      ED02
_   RACF Userid                    MYUSER
_   User's default group           CR540

    UNIX data
    UNIX user (uid)                54000_____
    UNIX home path                 /u/myuser_____
    Initial program                /bin/sh_____
    Max. address space size        _____
    Maximum CPU time               _____
    Max. files open per proc       _____
    Max. data space for mapping    _____
    Max. nr. of active procs       _____
    Max. nr. of active threads     _____
    Maximum non-shared memory      _____
    Maximum shared memory          _____
********************************* Bottom of Data ********************************
```

Figure 2.25   zSecure user OMVS segment

Information security is based on three processes: authentication, authorization, and auditing. In this chapter, you learned how to authenticate users and create identities so RACF can determine who is using the mainframe. In the next chapter, you learn how to use profiles and create authorizations so users can access specific data. Chapter 4, "Logging," covers auditing as a means to identify who did what and when.

2.5 Additional Information

The manuals contain a lot of additional information about users and groups. These books are particularly relevant:

- *z/OS Security Server RACF Security Administrator's Guide*, Chapter 3, "Defining Groups and Users"
- *z/OS Security Server RACF Command Language Reference*
- The zSecure Documentation at publib.boulder.ibm.com/infocenter/tivihelp/v2r1/index. jsp?topic=/com.ibm.zsecure.doc/welcome.htm

Protecting Data Sets and Other Resources

A production z/OS system using a mainframe can contain a wide variety of resources: data sets, UNIX file system files, databases, transactions, and so on. Information security is necessary to preserve the confidentiality, integrity, and availability of those resources. In this chapter, you learn how to configure profiles in RACF. Profiles specify the authorization level of users to determine who is authorized to read and modify resources such as those noted.

Most UNIX systems give all users similar permissions. Users who use just a specific application, such as the web server, are stored in a different user registry. Very often a single computer hosts only one application. On the other hand, a single z/OS mainframe can host a large number of applications, and the user registry can have everybody from users who are allowed to access only certain parts of a web site, to trusted administrators. Because of the diverse user population, it is vital to use profiles to limit resource access to authorized users.

3.1 Protecting Data Sets

Data sets are the z/OS equivalent of files and directories. In this section, you learn how to control the ability to access data sets for reading and writing.

3.1.1 Default Permissions

This example manipulates the permissions of the data set `<username>.RACFBK.CNTL`, which you created in Chapter 1, "Introduction to the Mainframe." To do this, define a RACF profile to set the permissions for access to the data set. This is similar to setting access controls using the `chmod` command in UNIX and to modifying the values in the Security tab in a file's properties in Windows.

Begin at the main RACF menu and choose option **1** for data set profiles. Next, choose option **1** to create a new profile. Optionally, typing **1.1** on the ISPF command line selects both options at the same time.

The RACF data set profile screen appears (see Figure 3.1).

The name of the profile is the same as the name of the data set it protects. Type the profile name **RACFBK.CNTL**, as shown in Figure 3.1, and press Enter. The user name is added automatically. You can leave the other fields empty.

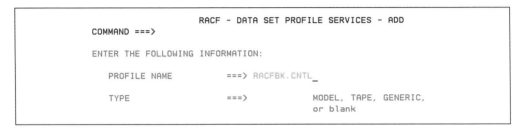

```
                                   RACF - DATA SET PROFILE SERVICES - ADD
              COMMAND ===>

              ENTER THE FOLLOWING INFORMATION:

                 PROFILE NAME          ===> RACFBK.CNTL_

                 TYPE                  ===>           MODEL, TAPE, GENERIC,
                                                      or blank
```

Figure 3.1   Adding a new profile

The default permission level in RACF is called UACC, for Universal Access Authority. In this exercise, the UACC is set to None so users cannot access the data set unless they are explicitly permitted to do so.

Table 3.1 shows the permission levels in RACF. The permissions are cumulative. For example, update permission includes read and execute permissions. These permissions apply to UACC and to explicit permission specifications, explained later in this chapter.

Table 3.1   RACF Permission Levels for Data Sets

Permission Level	Meaning
None	No permission
Execute	Can run the data set, if it is a binary executable (not an interpreted program—interpreted programs can be executed only if the interpreter has permission to read them)
Read	Can also read the contents of the data set
Update	Can also modify the content of the data set
Control	Can also modify the control interval of a VSAM data set
Alter	Can also alter the permissions for the data set, create it if it does not exist, and delete it if it does exist

VSAM

Virtual Storage Access Method, or VSAM, is the access method used for data sets that require random access, such as a list of bank accounts and their respective owners and balances. For more information about VSAM, see the IBM Redbook *VSAM Demystified.*

Do not specify any additional information at this time. The screen should look similar to that shown in Figure 3.2. Press Enter.

```
                         RACF - ADD DATA SET PROFILE
   COMMAND ===>

     PROFILE: RACFBK.CNTL

  ENTER OR CHANGE THE FOLLOWING INFORMATION:

     OWNER               ===> ORIPOME     Userid or group name
     LEVEL               ===> 0           0-99
     FAILED ACCESSES     ===> FAIL        FAIL or WARN
     UACC                ===> NONE        NONE, READ, UPDATE,
                                          CONTROL, ALTER or EXECUTE
```

Figure 3.2   Adding a data set profile

At this point, the UACC to the data set is NONE and there are no access control list (ACL) items to override it. This is equivalent to making a file inaccessible using chmod 000 <filename>. The data set should not be accessible to anybody without special permissions that are similar to root.

To determine whether the change in permission level was effective, open another terminal window. Log in as MYUSER, the user you created in Chapter 2, "Users and Groups." Attempt to edit <username>.RACFBK.CNTL(HELLOW), as shown in Figure 3.3.

```
                          Edit Entry Panel

    ISPF Library:
       Project . . . oripome
       Group . . . . racfbk     . . . _____  . . . _____  . . . _____
       Type  . . . . cntl
       Member  . . . hellow        (Blank or pattern for member selection list)
```

Figure 3.3   Attempt to edit <username>.RACFBK.CNTL(HELLOW) as MYUSER

The attempt to edit the data set should generate an error message, as shown in Figure 3.4.

```
  ICH408I USER(MYUSER  ) GROUP(OMVS    ) NAME(SAMPLE USER       )
    ORIPOME.RACFBK.CNTL CL(DATASET ) VOL(R01222)
    INSUFFICIENT ACCESS AUTHORITY
    ACCESS INTENT(READ   )  ACCESS ALLOWED(NONE   )
  IEC150I 913-38,IFG0194E,MYUSER,GENERAL,ISP22504,0501,R01222,ORIPOME.RACFBK.CNTL
  ***
```

Figure 3.4   Permission denied

MYUSER attempted to edit a data set without the proper permission level. Note that the error message shows the attempted access (the access intent) as read. The editor reads the data set member as soon as you try to access it, but attempts to write it only when you save or exit the editor.

An audit trail of RACF violations is kept. To view the audit record, return to the administrative user's terminal window (that's the regular user you use for most of the exercises). From the main ISPF menu, choose option **s** for the System Display and Search Facility. This is the same option used to view the output of JCL jobs in Chapter 1.

Within SDSF, type **log** to access the system log. Press F8 to scroll to the bottom of the log and F11 to scroll to the right. The log contains the same error message MYUSER sees, as shown in Figure 3.5.

```
   SDSF SYSLOG   3985.101 IPO1 IPO1 07/16/2007 0W    1839      COLUMNS  51 130
   COMMAND INPUT ===>                                          SCROLL ===> 1
  0281  $HASP100 MYUSER   ON TSOINRDR
  0090  $HASP373 MYUSER   STARTED
  0090  IEF125I MYUSER - LOGGED ON - TIME=11.38.22
  0090  ICH408I USER(MYUSER ) GROUP(OMVS    ) NAME(SAMPLE USER      ) 628
  0090    ORIPOME.RACFBK.CNTL CL(DATASET ) VOL(R01222)
  0090    INSUFFICIENT ACCESS AUTHORITY
  0090    ACCESS INTENT(READ   )   ACCESS ALLOWED(NONE   )
  0090  IEC150I 913-38,IFG0194E,MYUSER,GENERAL,ISP11381,0501,R01222,ORIPOME.RACF
        BK.CNTL
```

Figure 3.5   The message in the log

If you are having difficulties finding the message, use the find command. In this case, enter **find ich408i** in the command input field to search the system log for the error MYUSER generated. ICH408I messages are generated for every RACF violation.

Why the Log Is So Wide

The system log was not originally designed for terminals with 80 characters per line, but for line printers with 132 characters per line. This is why it is necessary to scroll to the right to view the entire error message.

To interpret this message, use the IBM LookAt search engine at http://www-03.ibm.com/servers/eserver/zseries/zos/bkserv/lookat. Type the message ID, **ICH408I**, and select the z/OS version.

Here's how this worked: The z/OS OPEN service (the equivalent to a system call in UNIX and Windows) called RACF to get permission for access. RACF figured that MYUSER should not be allowed access, so it issued the message ICH408I and told the OPEN service that access should be denied. OPEN then issued the message IEC150I, with the reason code 38, meaning that access was denied for security reasons.

3.1.2   Access Control List Permissions

If the HLQ (high-level qualifier, the part of the data set name until the first dot) is identical to a user's name, that user is allowed to do everything with the data set (read, edit, modify permissions, etc). It is possible to use a UACC for all other users. However, usually a higher degree of granularity is required. Access control lists (ACLs) provide this granularity. The UACC is the default access permission to be used only when nothing else is found to be applicable for a user attempting to access a resource.

The owner you set in the RACF data set profile is the owner of the profile that controls access, not the owner of the actual data set. In theory, this owner might not be able to access the information in the data set. He or she would be able to change the ACL to get access, but that action should be audited, and the owner might not have the capability to delete the audit trail.

The owner of the actual data set is the user or group whose name is the first component of the name of the data set. For example, `ORIPOME.RACFB.CNTL` is owned by the user ORIPOME. In most cases, this user has complete control of the data set.

To add an entry to the ACL, go to the RACF data set menu. Once there, choose option **2** to change a profile. The profile name is `RACFBK.CNTL`. Choose the option to change optional information by entering **yes**, as shown in Figure 3.6.

```
                          RACF - CHANGE DATA SET PROFILE
        COMMAND ===>

          PROFILE: RACFBK.CNTL

        ENTER THE DESIRED CHANGES:
            OWNER               ===>            Userid or group name
            LEVEL               ===>            0-99
            FAILED ACCESSES     ===>            FAIL or WARN
            UACC                ===>            NONE, READ, UPDATE,
                                                CONTROL, ALTER OR EXECUTE
            AUDIT SUCCESSES     ===>            READ, UPDATE, CONTROL,
                                                ALTER, or NOAUDIT
            AUDIT FAILURES      ===>            READ, UPDATE, CONTROL,
                                                ALTER, or NOAUDIT
            REMOVE NOTIFY       ===>            YES or blank
            NOTIFY USER         ===>            Userid
            ERASE ON DELETE     ===>            YES, NO or blank
            RETENTION PERIOD    ===>            (Tape only) 0-65533 (days)
                                                or 99999 (for never expires)


        TO CHANGE OPTIONAL INFORMATION, ENTER YES     ===> yes _
```

Figure 3.6   Changing a data set profile

Select the access list by entering **yes**, as shown in Figure 3.7.

```
                          RACF - CHANGE DATA SET PROFILE
    COMMAND ===>

       PROFILE: RACFBK.CNTL

    TO CHANGE THE FOLLOWING INFORMATION, ENTER YES:

       VOLUMES                              ===>
       SECURITY LEVEL OR CATEGORIES         ===>
       SECURITY LABEL                       ===>
       INSTALLATION DATA                    ===>
       DFP-RELATED PARAMETERS               ===>
       ACCESS LIST                          ===> yes _
```

Figure 3.7   Choosing what to change

Next, choose option **1** to add a user to the access control list, as shown in Figure 3.8.

```
                          RACF - MAINTAIN DATA SET ACCESS LIST
    OPTION ===> 1_

       PROFILE: RACFBK.CNTL

    SELECT ONE OF THE FOLLOWING:

       1  ADD      Add users or groups.
                   Copy the access list from an existing profile.


       2  REMOVE   Remove specific users and groups from the access list.


       3  RESET    Remove all users and groups from the access list.
```

Figure 3.8   Adding an ACL entry

Enter **yes** in the second field to specify the users and groups to be added to the access list, as shown in Figure 3.9. Later you might find it useful to use the other option to copy an existing access control list from a different profile.

Enter the authority level (read) and the name of the user with the permission level (MYUSER), as shown in Figure 3.10. Press Enter to accept access changes.

From the terminal window where you are logged on as MYUSER, try again to edit <username>.RACFBK.CNTL(HELLOW). It will work. Try to save the modified data set using the save command, as shown in Figure 3.11.

```
                         RACF - MAINTAIN DATA SET ACCESS LIST - ADD
   COMMAND ===>

      PROFILE: RACFBK.CNTL

   ENTER YES FOR EITHER OR BOTH OF THE FOLLOWING:


      COPY        ===> NO      YES to copy the access list from another
                               profile.


      SPECIFY     ===> yes _   YES to specify the users and groups to be
                               added to the access list.
```

Figure 3.9   Choosing to specify users and groups

```
                         RACF - MAINTAIN DATA SET ACCESS LIST - ADD
   COMMAND ===>

      PROFILE: RACFBK.CNTL

   Enter the access authority to be granted:

      AUTHORITY        ===> read      NONE, READ, UPDATE,
                                      CONTROL, ALTER or EXECUTE

   Enter the users or groups for which entries are to be added:

      ===> myuser_  ===>         ===>         ===>         ===>
      ===>          ===>         ===>         ===>         ===>
```

Figure 3.10   Specifying users and groups

```
   EDIT       ORIPOME.RACFBK.CNTL(HELLOW) - 01.00          Columns 00001 00072
   ****** ***************************** Top of Data ******************************:
   ==MSG> -Warning- The UNDO command is not available until you change
   ==MSG>           your edit profile using the command RECOVERY ON.
   000100 //TSOJOB   JOB CLASS=A,NOTIFY=&SYSUID,MSGCLASS=H
   000200 //        EXEC PGM=IKJEFT01
   000300 //SYSTSPRT DD SYSOUT=*
   000400 //SYSTSIN  DD *
   000500 SEND 'Hello, world' U(ORIPOME) .
   000600 /*
   ****** ***************************** Bottom of Data ****************************:




   Command ===> save_____ Scroll ===> PAGE
```

Figure 3.11   Attempting to save <username>.RACFBK.CNTL(HELLOW) as MYUSER

The attempt to save the modified data set member will fail, as shown in Figure 3.12. The attempt fails because the access authority is limited to read. Update authority is not permitted.

```
ICH408I USER(MYUSER  ) GROUP(OMVS    ) NAME(SAMPLE USER          )
  ORIPOME.RACFBK.CNTL CL(DATASET ) VOL(R01222)
  INSUFFICIENT ACCESS AUTHORITY
  ACCESS INTENT(UPDATE )  ACCESS ALLOWED(READ    )
IEC150I 913-38,IFG0194E,MYUSER,GENERAL,ISP23191,0501,R01222,ORIPOME.RACFBK.CNTL
***  _
```

Figure 3.12   Save failure

To edit from the editor, enter the command **cancel**. If you made any changes, you might need to press Enter to confirm the cancellation.

In preparation for later exercises, you need to remove MYUSER from the access list for the resource. We show you how to do this from the command line so that you will learn the command-line interface, too.

As you recall from the previous chapter, RACF commands are documented in the manual *z/OS Security Server RACF Command Language Reference* (see Chapter 5). The relevant commands are LISTDSD, which lists a data set profile, and PERMIT, which alters ACLs.

At the TSO READY prompt, run this command to list the data set profile, including the ACL:

LISTDSD DATASET(RACFBK.CNTL) AUTHUSER

The DATASET parameter on the LISTDSD command specifies the data set profile to examine. Alternatively, you can use the shortened version:

LD DA(RACFBK.CNTL) AUTHUSER

The AUTHUSER parameter specifies to display the access list. Figure 3.13 shows the relevant part of the output.

```
SECLABEL
--------
NO SECLABEL

   ID     ACCESS    ACCESS COUNT
--------  -------   -------------
MYUSER     READ        00000

   ID    ACCESS  ACCESS COUNT  CLASS         ENTITY NAME
-------- ------- ------------- --------  ------------------------------------------
NO ENTRIES IN CONDITIONAL ACCESS LIST
```

Figure 3.13   The ACL LISTDSD returns

For more information about LISTDSD, see the manual at *z/OS V1R6.0 Security Server RACF Command Language Reference*, Topic 5.13, "LISTDSD (List Data Set Profile)," or the equivalent for other z/OS versions. Alternatively, you can issue `HELP LISTDSD` from the TSO prompt.

To modify the ACL, use the `PERMIT` command. The following command deletes `MYUSER` from the ACL for `RACFBK.CNTL`. `MYUSER`'s access after this command depends on the UACC and any groups to which `MYUSER` belongs that appear in the ACL.

`PERMIT RACFBK.CNTL DELETE ID(MYUSER)`

For more information about `PERMIT`, see the manual at *z/OS V1R6.0 Security Server RACF Command Language Reference*, Topic 5.17, "PERMIT (Maintain Resource Access Lists)," or the equivalent for other z/OS versions. Alternatively, you can issue `HELP PERMIT` from the TSO prompt.

You can repeat the `LISTDSD` command to see that the access list is now empty. If you are truly paranoid (and, as a security professional, you are supposed to be), log on as MYUSER and verify that you cannot read the data set any longer.

3.1.3 Project Groups and Generic Profiles

In this example, we create a group profile to manage mainframe library information. Everyone should have read access to the library information because it contains information to be referenced by all mainframe users. It is not necessary to use a group in this scenario, but we expect eventually to have a team of librarians allowed to modify the library data sets—and it will be easier to accommodate that if the data sets are grouped together.

The first step is to create a group profile called TEXTS. Choose option **3** from the RACF menu. Type the group name, **TEXTS**, and then select option **1** to add the group profile.

Enter the owner as your user ID and the superior group as **SYS1** (a group that is created by default during z/OS installation). Leave the other fields as the default values, as shown in Figure 3.14.

```
                        RACF - ADD GROUP TEXTS
     COMMAND ===>

     Enter the following information:

         OWNER                      ===> ORIPOME     Userid or group name
         SUPERIOR GROUP             ===> SYS1_
         USE TERMINAL UACC          ===> YES         YES or NO
         UNIVERSAL ATTRIBUTE        ===> NO          YES or NO
```

Figure 3.14 Creating the TEXTS group

Generic profiles are profiles that apply to every data set that matches a specific expression. For example, if all users on the mainframe should be allowed to read TEXTS data sets that begin with B, create a data set profile with the name `'TEXTS.B*.*'` of type GENERIC, as shown in Figure 3.15, to specify the permission. Under the ISPF naming conventions, TEXTS is the project name, B* matches every group name that starts with a B, and the final * matches the data set type in most cases. Some data set types have another component beyond the type, in which case this generic profile will not match them. To cover those, use double asterisk (**), as explained shortly.

Note

The name of the profile is enclosed in apostrophes because otherwise the system would automatically add the name of the current user to the beginning of the profile name.

```
                          RACF - DATA SET PROFILE SERVICES - ADD
   COMMAND ===>

   ENTER THE FOLLOWING INFORMATION:

      PROFILE NAME          ===> 'TEXTS.B*.*'

      TYPE                  ===> generic _   MODEL, TAPE, GENERIC,
                                             or blank
```

Figure 3.15   Creating the generic profile

Everyone requires read access to these data sets, so set the default UACC to read. Set both audit levels to read so that RACF will audit any type of access attempt to these files, as shown in Figure 3.16. Press Enter to create the profile.

```
                          RACF - ADD DATA SET PROFILE
   COMMAND ===>

      PROFILE: 'TEXTS.B*.*'

   ENTER OR CHANGE THE FOLLOWING INFORMATION:

         OWNER               ===> ORIPOME     Userid or group name
         LEVEL               ===> 0           0-99
         FAILED ACCESSES     ===> FAIL        FAIL or WARN
         UACC                ===> read        NONE, READ, UPDATE,
                                              CONTROL, ALTER or EXECUTE
         AUDIT SUCCESSES     ===> read    _   READ, UPDATE, CONTROL,
                                              ALTER, or NOAUDIT
         AUDIT FAILURES      ===> READ        READ, UPDATE, CONTROL,
                                              ALTER, or NOAUDIT
```

Figure 3.16   Generic profile information

Return to the main menu and create two library data sets. You can get to that screen by entering the command **=3.2**, which moves back to the main ISPF menu; then choose option **3**, utilities from the main ISPF menu, followed by option **2**, data set utilities. Allocate a new data set in the TEXTS project called `Books`, of type `TEXT`, as shown in Figure 3.17.

```
                                Data Set Utility
        Option ===> A

            A Allocate new data set          C Catalog data set
            R Rename entire data set         U Uncatalog data set
            D Delete entire data set         S Short data set information
        blank Data set information           V VSAM Utilities

        ISPF Library:
            Project  . . texts           Enter "/" to select option
            Group  . . . books           /  Confirm Data Set Delete
            Type . . . . text
```

Figure 3.17   Creating a new data set

Leave all the parameters on the next screen as their default values and press Enter. Then create another data set called `TEXTS.USERS.TEXT`. In contrast to the previous data set, this one will not be affected by the generic profile.

Next, choose option **2** from the main ISPF menu and use the editor to create the members `TEXTS.BOOKS.TEXT(DESC)` and `TEXTS.USERS.TEXT(DESC)`. In each member, enter a short line to describe the data set.

In the other terminal window, where you are logged on as MYUSER, try to edit `TEXTS.BOOKS.TEXT(DESC)`. The edit is permitted, but the save fails, as shown in Figure 3.18.

```
        ICH408I USER(MYUSER  ) GROUP(OMVS    ) NAME(SAMPLE USER          )
          TEXTS.BOOKS.TEXT CL(DATASET ) VOL(RO1223)
          INSUFFICIENT ACCESS AUTHORITY
          FROM TEXTS.B*.* (G)
          ACCESS INTENT(UPDATE )  ACCESS ALLOWED(READ  )
        IEC150I 913-38,IFG0194E,MYUSER,GENERAL,ISP23181,0502,RO1223,TEXTS.BOOKS.TEXT
        *** _
```

Figure 3.18   Saving the changes fails

Exit the editor. F3 does not exit because it automatically tries to save the file. Instead, enter the command **cancel**. If you made any changes, you might need to press Enter to confirm the cancellation.

Now try to edit `TEXTS.USERS.TEXT(DESC)`. MYUSER might be able to edit and save the changes. This data set is not covered by any profile, so it is protected by the default behavior. This default behavior is specified as the `PROTECTALL` option. To see the value of `PROTECTALL`, run this command:

```
SETR LIST
```

The relevant line starts with PROTECT-ALL, as shown in Figure 3.19.

```
JES-EARLYVERIFY OPTION IS INACTIVE
PROTECT-ALL OPTION IS NOT IN EFFECT
TAPE DATA SET PROTECTION IS INACTIVE
```

Figure 3.19   PROTECTALL setting in the output of SETR LIST

PROTECTALL has three possible settings:

- **NOPROTECTALL**—Access is open by default. Access is always allowed unless there is a protection profile.

- **PROTECTALL(WARN)**—If there is no protection profile, access is allowed, but with a warning to the user and the security administrator.

- **PROTECTALL(FAIL)**—Access is closed by default. Access is always denied unless a protection profile allows it. This is the proper setting for a production system.

To avoid this "open by default" scenario for the TEXTS project, create a new generic profile called 'TEXTS.**'. Set the UACC value to none as the default permission level for this profile. The asterisk (*) matches one component of the data set name. Data set name components are separated by periods. In contrast, the double asterisk (**) can match any number of components.

This operation fails if the EGN (enhanced generic names) option is disabled. In such a case, you can create a profile 'TEXTS.*.*' or run this command to enable it:

SETR EGN

Choose option **D** (for *display*) from the data set profile services menu to see which data sets the new profile protects. The first screen displays the name of the new profile by default. In the second screen, enter **yes** next to data sets to see the names of the protected data sets, as shown in Figure 3.20.

```
                        RACF - DISPLAY DATA SET PROFILE
    COMMAND ===>

      PROFILE: 'TEXTS.**'

   TO SELECT INFORMATION TO BE DISPLAYED, ENTER YES:

      ACCESS LIST  ===>             Profile access list
      HISTORY      ===>             Profile history
      STATISTICS   ===>             Profile use statistics
      DFP          ===>             Profile DFP information
      DATA SETS    ===> yes _       Protected data sets
      NO RACF      ===>             Limit the display to the selected
                                    information.
```

Figure 3.20   Asking for protected data sets

The profile information fills more than one screen. Press F8 to scroll down and verify that TEXTS.USERS.TEXT is protected, as shown in Figure 3.21.

```
   BROWSE - RACF COMMAND OUTPUT---------------------- LINE 00000020 COL 001 080
   COMMAND ===> _                                          SCROLL ===> PAGE
 -----------          '
   NONE

NO INSTALLATION DATA

CATALOGUED DATA SETS AFFECTED BY PROFILE CHANGE
----------------------------------------------
TEXTS.USERS.TEXT
******************************** Bottom of Data ********************************
```

Figure 3.21   Data sets protected by a generic profile

Notice that even though TEXTS.** matches TEXTS.BOOKS.TEXT, this generic profile does not protect it. When multiple profiles apply to a data set, the most specific one is used. TEXTS.B*.* is more specific than TEXTS.**. A discrete profile for a data set always takes priority over a generic profile, even when the generic profile has the same name.

3.2 Other Resources

We now use z/OS UNIX System Services resources to demonstrate how to protect resources that are not data sets. In contrast to UNIX, z/OS does not operate on the concept that everything is a file (or a data set). To protect other resources, you must create a profile with the appropriate resource class. The resource class identifies the type of the resource.

UNIX systems make a distinction between root and nonroot users. Mainframe permission levels allow a more granular approach. You can provide users some of the root privileges without giving them full control of the system.

3.2.1 Gathering Information

You need to know how to use RACF to manage z/OS UNIX permissions and what each permission allows users to do. We could list the options in this book, but that would defeat the purpose of this section: to teach you to use authorization for *any* mainframe resource. Too many resource types exist to teach them all in this book.

Protecting resources is part of the role of a security administrator. Therefore, the place to look is the manual *z/OS Security Server RACF Security Administrator's Guide*. In that manual, Chapter 20 deals with z/OS UNIX, and Topic 20.7 deals with managing z/OS UNIX privileges, as shown in Figure 3.22.

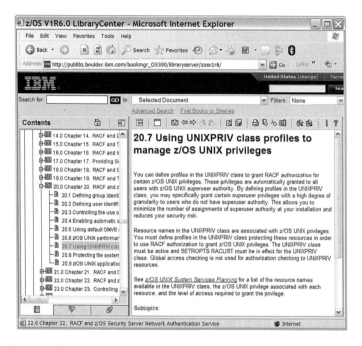

Figure 3.22   Topic 20.7 in the *Security Administrator's Guide*—UNIX privileges

This section specifies that the information is in the *z/OS UNIX System Services Planning Guide*. Within that manual for z/OS Version 1.6, you'll find the list of UNIXPRIV class profiles in Topic 5.5, as shown in Figure 3.23.

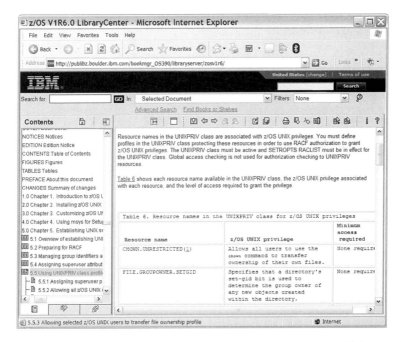

Figure 3.23 The UNIXPRIV resources in Topic 5.5 of the *z/OS V1R6.0 UNIX System Services Planning Guide*

3.2.2 Activating UNIXPRIV

To manage z/OS UNIX privileges, you need to use the UNIXPRIV class. To use UNIXPRIV, you must take the following actions (as documented in the *z/OS UNIX System Services Planning Guide*):

1. Ensure that the UNIXPRIV class is active.

2. Ensure that SETROPTS RACLIST is in effect for the UNIXPRIV class.

3. Create a profile.

The first two are global operations. To verify, navigate to the main RACF menu and choose option 5 for system options; then choose 1 to display the current status of options.

If UNIXPRIV is configured, it will be displayed in the ACTIVE CLASS list, as shown in Figure 3.24.

```
ACTIVE CLASSES = DATASET USER GROUP ACCTNUM CBIND CIMS DIMS FACILITY FIELD
                 GXFACILI LOGSTRM PTKTDATA PTKTVAL RODMMGR SERVER STARTED
                 TSOAUTH TSOPROC UNIXPRIV XFACILIT
GENERIC PROFILE CLASSES =  DATASET CBIND CIMS FACILITY SERVER STARTED
                           XFACILIT
GENERIC COMMAND CLASSES =  DATASET CBIND CIMS FACILITY SERVER STARTED
                           XFACILIT
```

Figure 3.24   UNIXPRIV is active and has SET RACLIST

If UNIXPRIV is not active, select option **3** (class options) and change it for specific classes, as shown in Figure 3.25.

```
                           RACF - SET CLASS OPTIONS
      COMMAND ===>


      To CHANGE options for  ALL  CLASSES on your system, enter YES or
      NO for any of the following types of SETROPTS options:

        ACTIVE              ===>      YES to activate, NO to deactivate
        STATISTICS          ===>      YES to activate, NO to deactivate
        GLOBAL              ===>      YES to activate, NO to deactivate
        GENERIC             ===>      YES to activate, NO to deactivate
        GENERIC COMMANDS    ===>      YES to activate, NO to deactivate


   To CHANGE options for SPECIFIC CLASSES,
        enter YES      ===> yes
```

Figure 3.25   Choosing to change specific classes

Enter the name of the class, **UNIXPRIV**. Enter **yes** in the ACTIVE and RACLIST columns, as shown in Figure 3.26.

```
                           RACF - SET CLASS OPTIONS
      COMMAND ===>

      To ACTIVATE options, enter YES.
      To DEACTIVATE options, enter NO.


                                                  GENERIC
        CLASS      ACTIVE  STATISTICS  GLOBAL  GENERIC  COMMANDS  RACLIST  GENLIST

        unixpriv   yes     ____        ____     ____     ____     yes _     ____
        ____       ____    ____        ____     ____     ____     ____      ____
```

Figure 3.26   Configuring the UNIXPRIV class

What Is RACLIST?

RACLIST is a RACF option that controls the caching of profiles. With RACLIST turned on, the profiles for that class, such as `UNIXPRIV`, are stored in memory (or virtual memory) and shared by different users running on the system. This improves performance.

Note that the profile cache does not refresh automatically. When you change the RACF profiles, you need to issue the refresh command for the changes to take effect.

For more information about this subject, see the *z/OS V1R6.0 Security Server RACF Security Administrator's Guide*, Topic 5.3.2.

3.2.3 Delegating `chown` Privileges

Typically in UNIX, a user is either authorized to use `su` to become the super user or not. In Windows, the equivalent operation is to be a member of the Power User and/or Administrators groups. RACF allows much more finely grained control of root privileges. You learn most of the details about controlling RACF itself in Chapter 6, "Limited-Authority RACF Administrators." In this section, you learn how to allow a user to use some root privileges in UNIX System Services without allowing all root access. To do this, you use the `UNIXPRIV` class to enable MYUSER to change files' ownership. MYUSER will not have any of the other root privileges, such as the capability to read any file or to terminate processes.

Topic 5.5 in the *z/OS V1R6.0 UNIX System Services Planning Guide* contains a table with the profile names for the `UNIXPRIV` class. As an exercise, you will use one of those profiles, `SUPERUSER.FILESYS.CHOWN`, to enable MYUSER to change file ownership. This change will not give MYUSER any other privileges.

From the main RACF menu, select option **2** to create a general resource profile (any profile that is not for data sets). Select option **1** to add a new profile. The class for the new profile must be `UNIXPRIV`. The profile is named after the permission it grants, `SUPERUSER.FILESYS.CHOWN`, as shown in Figure 3.27.

```
                        RACF - GENERAL RESOURCE SERVICES -  ADD
   OPTION ===>

 ENTER THE FOLLOWING PROFILE INFORMATION:

    CLASS     ===> UNIXPRIV

    PROFILE   ===> superuser.filesys.chown_
```

Figure 3.27   Creating a general profile

Leave all the information as the default values, and specify **yes** to add optional information. Type any key next to `ACCESS LIST` to specify the access list. Select option **1** to add users,
and then select to specify the users, as shown in Figure 3.28.

```
                    RACF - MAINTAIN GENERAL RESOURCE ACCESS LIST - ADD
        COMMAND ===>

          CLASS:          UNIXPRIV
          PROFILE       _ superuser.filesys.chown


        ENTER YES FOR EITHER OR BOTH OF THE FOLLOWING:

          COPY          ===>          YES to copy the access list from another
                                      profile.

          SPECIFY       ===> yes      YES to specify the users and groups to be
                                      added to the access list.
```

Figure 3.28   Choosing to specify the users to add to the access list

According to Section 5.5 of the *z/OS UNIX System Services Planning Guide,* the minimum
access level required for `SUPERUSER.FILESYS.CHOWN` is read. This means that a user must be
granted at least read permission on this profile to be able to run the `chown` command. Specify
read as the authority level for MYUSER, as shown in Figure 3.29.

```
                    RACF - MAINTAIN GENERAL RESOURCE ACCESS LIST - ADD
        COMMAND ===>

          CLASS:          UNIXPRIV
          PROFILE       __ superuser.filesys.chown


        Enter the access authority to be granted:

          AUTHORITY     ===> read      NONE, READ, UPDATE,
                                       CONTROL, ALTER or EXECUTE

        Enter the users or groups for which entries are to be added:

          ===> myuser_  ===>        ===>        ===>        ===>
          ===>          ===>        ===>        ===>        ===>
```

Figure 3.29   Adding MYUSER to the access list

After you enter the values, the profile is added. Depending on the RACLIST settings, the
changes might not be effective until a `SETROPTS  REFRESH` command is issued. Issue this
command:

```
TSO SETROPTS REFRESH RACLIST(UNIXPRIV)
```

This command refreshes the cache, the in-memory version of the RACF permission settings, for the `UNIXPRIV` class. The `TSO` at the beginning of the command example specifies for ISPF that it is a TSO command.

3.2.4 Verifying the Change

After you update the cache with `SETROPTS REFRESH`, the RACF cache has the added profile. Next, verify that the change works as expected. Use the terminal window where you are logged in as MYUSER. From the main ISPF menu, run OMVS. You can run it directly from the option line:

```
tso omvs
```

Then run the following UNIX commands to create a file and change its ownership:

```
touch testfile
ls -l testfile
chown omvskern testfile
ls -l testfile
```

This changes the owner of `testfile` to OMVSKERN, the root user for UNIX System Services. The window should look similar to the one shown in Figure 3.30.

```
    MYUSER:/u/myuser>touch testfile
    MYUSER:/u/myuser>ls -l testfile
    -rw-r--r--   1 MYUSER    CBCFG1          0 Feb 13 14:11 testfile
    MYUSER:/u/myuser>chown omvskern testfile
    MYUSER:/u/myuser>ls -l testfile
    -rw-r--r--   1 OMVSKERN CBCFG1           0 Feb 13 14:11 testfile
    MYUSER:/u/myuser>
```

Figure 3.30   Changing file ownership

3.2.5 Deleting Resource Profiles

As the last exercise in this section, use the command-line interface to delete the `SUPERUSER.FILESYS.CHOWN` profile in the `UNIXPRIV` class to remove MYUSER's privilege. Run this command at the `READY` prompt or by preceding it with TSO from the ISPF command line:

```
RDELETE UNIXPRIV SUPERUSER.FILESYS.CHOWN
```

Then refresh the `RACLIST` for `UNIXPRIV`. This operation is also called doing a `SETROPTS RACLIST REFRESH` on the `UNIXPRIV` class.

```
SETROPTS REFRESH RACLIST(UNIXPRIV)
```

3.3 Security Data (Levels, Categories, and Labels)

You've seen several ways to give users access to resources that are based solely on the identity of the person accessing the resource. Consider the access list entry: If you are on the access list with the correct level of authority or in a group that is on the access list with the correct level of authority, you are allowed access to the data.

You can also control access to data based on the characteristics of the data and the user by assigning a security level and one or more categories to the user and the data.

Warning

Security labels and categories can be useful in controlling access to data. However, they are discretionary access controls, in the sense that once the data is accessible by the user, the user can reclassify the data, potentially to a lower (or no) sensitivity level or a different set of categories—possibly the empty set.

3.3.1 Defining the Policy

To activate security data checking, run this command:

```
SETR CLASSACT(SECDATA)
```

3.3.1.1 Security Levels

A security level is a hierarchical classification of the sensitivity level of a resource. For example, if you have a data set that anyone is allowed to access, you might assign that data set the security level of PUBLIC. A data set that is allowed only to employees could be assigned the security level of EMPONLY. Confidential information could be assigned the security level of CORPCONF. These levels are hierarchical, in the sense that CORPCONF is more sensitive than EMPONLY, which is, in turn, more sensitive than PUBLIC.

RACF implements security levels by allowing you to define labels such as PUBLIC, EMPONLY, and CORPCONF, and assigning them a numeric value between 1 and 255, which represents the level of sensitivity.

All of an installation's security levels are defined in the SECLEVEL profile in the RACF SECDATA general resource class. The z/OS security administrator defines these profiles using the RDEFINE command.

This command creates the security levels profile:

```
RDEFINE SECDATA SECLEVEL
```

This command adds security levels. It implements the three security levels explained previously:

```
RALTER SECDATA SECLEVEL ADDMEM(PUBLIC/10 EMPONLY/50 CORPCONF/100)
```

This is the command to use to list the security levels:

```
RLIST SECDATA SECLEVEL
```

3.3.1.2 Categories

You can also assign one or more categories to a resource. A category is a description of the information contained in the resource. For example, FINANCIAL, DESIGN, and TEST could all be categories. With categories, no hierarchical relationship exists: The operating system can't tell from the category name which category is more sensitive.

All of an installation's categories are defined in the CATEGORY profile in the RACF SECDATA general resource class. The z/OS security administrator defines these profiles using the RDEFINE command, as shown here.

This command creates the new categories profile:

```
RDEFINE SECDATA CATEGORY UACC(NONE)
```

This command adds categories:

```
RALTER SECDATA CATEGORY ADDMEM(FINANCIAL DESIGN TEST)
```

This is the command to use to list the categories:

```
RLIST SECDATA CATEGORY
```

3.3.2 Assigning Security Levels and Categories

Just defining the security levels and categories does nothing to change who is allowed access to what resources. You must assign levels or categories to users and resources. After that, access to the resource is allowed only under these conditions:

1. The user has been assigned a security level that is not lower than the security level of the sources.
2. The user has been assigned all the categories that are assigned to the resource.

Security levels are assigned to users using either the RACF panels or the RACF commands. For example, this RACF ALTUSER command can be used to assign the security label EMPONLY and the categories DESIGN and TEST to the user ID MYUSER:

```
ALTUSER MYUSER SECLEVEL(EMPONLY) ADDCATEGORY(DESIGN TEST)
```

You can also assign categories and levels to data sets using either the RACF panels or the RACF commands. This is the RACF ALTDSD command to add the security level CORPCONF and the category TEST to the data set RACFBK.CNTL:

```
ALTDSD RACFBK.CNTL SECLEVEL(CORPCONF) ADDCATEGORY(TEST)
```

Now add MYUSER to the ACL for RACFBK.CNTL:

```
PERMIT RACFBK.CNTL ACCESS(READ) ID(MYUSER)
```

MYUSER should not have access to RACFBK.CNTL, despite the ACL, because of the security level. Log on as MYUSER and try to edit <your user name>.RACFBK.CNTL(HELLOW). You will get the error shown in Figure 3.31.

```
ICH408I USER(MYUSER  ) GROUP(OMVS    ) NAME(SAMPLE USER        )
  ORIPOME.RACFBK.CNTL CL(DATASET ) VOL(R01222)
  INSUFFICIENT SECURITY LEVEL/CATEGORY AUTHORITY
  ACCESS INTENT(READ  )  ACCESS ALLOWED(NONE   )
IEC150I 913-38,IFG0194E,MYUSER,GENERAL,ISP16271,0501,R01222,ORIPOME.RACFBK.CNTL
  ***  _
```

Figure 3.31   Access denied because of security level

To allow access, run this command to modify MYUSER's security level:

```
ALTUSER MYUSER SECLEVEL(CORPCONF)
```

Log off as MYUSER and log back on. Now MYUSER should be able to read the data set member in the editor.

Note

The security level of a user is cached during a TSO session. Therefore, it is necessary to log MYUSER off and then back on before the new security level takes effect.

3.3.3 Security Labels (SECLABELs)

Security labels (SECLABELs) are a means of aggregating security levels and categories into a single entity that can be assigned to users and resources. Using SECLABELs allows an installation to protect against the data owner or the user of the data using their discretionary access control (DAC) authority to change the classification or categorization of data. By controlling these discretionary powers, you can move your installation into a mandatory access control (MAC) environment. Moving into MAC allows the safe concurrent processing of multiple levels of security within the same computing environment. This is called Multilevel Security (MLS). This enables an organization to set rules on data access that the data and application administrators cannot override. The authority to modify those data access rules can be limited to a small number of trusted security administrators.

Although MAC environments are often thought of as being of interest only to three-letter government agencies, there is significant commercial benefit to a MAC environment. For example, if a company wants to isolate information from different divisions or has information that must not be divulged across some IT boundary, an MLS environment could be an excellent solution.

To activate security labels, run these commands:

```
SETR CLASSACT(SECLABEL)
```

```
SETR RACLIST(SECLABEL)
```

SECLABELs are profiles within the RACF `SECLABEL` general resource class. SECLABELs can be defined with the `RDEFINE RACF` command. For example, this command defines a SECLABEL called `FINCONF`:

```
RDEFINE SECLABEL FINCONF SECLEVEL(CORPCONF) ADDCATEGORY(FINANCIAL)
  UACC(NONE)
```

After the SECLABEL is defined, you assign it to resources using either the RACF panels or the RACF commands. For example, to assign the `FINCONF` SECLABEL to `<username>`. `RACFBK.CNTL`, use this `ALTDSD` command:

```
ALTDSD RACFBK.CNTL SECLABEL(FINCONF)
```

This command classifies `RACFBK.CNTL` as having "FINCONF" data. After you run it, MYUSER would fail to access `<username>.RACFBK.CNTL` and would see the error message shown in Figure 3.32.

```
   ICH408I USER(MYUSER  ) GROUP(OMVS    ) NAME(SAMPLE USER        )
     ORIPOME.RACFBK.CNTL CL(DATASET ) VOL(RO1222)
     INSUFFICIENT SECURITY LABEL AUTHORITY
     ACCESS INTENT(READ   )  ACCESS ALLOWED(NONE   )
   IEC150I 913-38,IFG0194E,MYUSER,GENERAL,ISP16572,0501,RO1222,ORIPOME.RACFBK.CNTL
   ***
```

Figure 3.32   Access denied because of security label

To grant MYUSER the right to access resources that have the `FINCONF` SECLABEL, modify the ACL to give it read access to the SECLABEL. These commands specify that MYUSER is allowed to access `FINCONF` classified information.

```
PERMIT FINCONF CLASS(SECLABEL) ID(MYUSER) ACCESS(READ) SETROPTS
  REFRESH RACLIST(SECLABEL)
```

When users start their work, they need to identify what SECLABEL is to be used. For TSO users, this is done on the TSO LOGON panel, as shown in Figure 3.33. For batch jobs, this is done using the SECLABEL JCL keyword. Other environments have their own ways of specifying what SECLABEL is to be assigned to the work.

```
----------------------------- TSO/E LOGON --------------------------------


    Enter LOGON parameters below:              RACF LOGON parameters:

    Userid   ===> MYUSER                       Seclabel    ===> finconf_

    Password ===>                              New Password ===>
```

Figure 3.33   TSO logon with SECLABEL

3.4 Securing UNIX System Services (USS) Files

In USS, an entire file system is stored in a single z/OS data set. To see the data sets that are mounted as file systems, use the df command, as shown in Figure 3.34. Obviously, the different files on each file system must have different permissions.

```
ORIPOME:/u/oripome>df
Mounted on     Filesystem                Avail/Total    Files       Status
/usr/lpp/java/J5.0_64 (AJV.V5ROM064.HFS)      88600/576000   4294966045 Availa
ble
/usr/lpp/java/J5.0 (AJV.V5ROM0.HFS)         58920/576000   4294966045 Available
/usr/lpp/java/J1.4_64 (AJV.V1R4M064.HFS)      51808/432000   4294966302 Availa
ble
/usr/lpp/java/J1.4 (AJV.V1R4M0.HFS)         37976/432000   4294966283 Available
/usr/lpp/java  (AJV.V1R1M0.HFS)         36872/662400   4294966135 Available
/SYSTEM/var     (OMVS.VAR)           16456/17280    4294967234 Available
/SYSTEM/tmp     (OMVS.TMP)           16720/17280    4294967269 Available
/SYSTEM/etc     (OMVS.ETC)           14408/17280    4294967046 Available
/SYSTEM/dev     (OMVS.DEV)            9896/10080    4294967283 Available
/usr/lpp/db2    (DSN.V7R1M0.SDSNHFS)   1912/28800    4294967223 Available
/u/WebSphere390/CB390 (OMVS.WAS.CONFIG.HFS)    22048/28800    4294967051 Availa
ble
/u             (OMVS.U)             15800/17280    4294967238 Available
/              (OMVS160D.ROOT)     129224/3296064 4294956608 Available
```

Figure 3.34   Data sets used as USS file systems

USS supports the standard UNIX security model, with different permissions for a file's owner, a file's group, and everybody else. In addition to using ls -l, you can view the permissions using getfacl. Run these commands:

```
touch acl_test
chmod 640 acl_test
ls -l acl_test
getfacl acl_test
```

The output should be similar to that shown in Figure 3.35.

```
ORIPOME:/u/oripome>touch acl_test
ORIPOME:/u/oripome>chmod 640 acl_test
ORIPOME:/u/oripome>ls -l acl_test
-rw-r-----  1 ORIPOME  CBCFG1         0 Jul 30 08:53 acl_test
ORIPOME:/u/oripome>getfacl acl_test
#file:  acl_test
#owner: ORIPOME
#group: CBCFG1
user::rw-
group::r--
other::---
```

Figure 3.35   Normal UNIX permissions in USS

In addition to the standard UNIX model, USS supports ACLs. These ACLs are controlled using the `setfacl` command. To allow MYUSER to read `acl_test`, run this command:

`setfacl -m user:MYUSER:r-- acl_test`

Now the `getfacl` results should show the new entry in the ACL, as you can see in Figure 3.36.

```
ORIPOME:/u/oripome>setfacl -m user:MYUSER:r-- acl_test
ORIPOME:/u/oripome>getfacl acl_test
#file:  acl_test
#owner: ORIPOME
#group: CBCFG1
user::rw-
group::r--
other::---
user:MYUSER:r--
```

Figure 3.36   USS ACL with an added user

Log on to OMVS as MYUSER to verify that you can read `acl_test` (it should be empty) but not write to it. USS ACL checks require the FSSEC class to be active. If MYUSER cannot read `acl_test`, run this TSO command to activate it and try again:

`SETR CLASSACT(FSSEC)`

To delete the ACL entry, use this command:

`setfacl -x user:MYUSER acl_test`

For more information, run `man setfacl` and `man getfacl`.

3.5 zSecure

In zSecure, you use RA.D to manipulate data set profiles, and RA.R to manipulate general resource profiles. To view the profiles that match particular criteria, enter those criteria in the data set selection panel. For example, Figure 3.37 shows a search for all the data set profiles that start with OMVS.

```
                          zSecure Suite - RACF - Data set Selection
          Command ===> _____  _ start panel

          _   Add new DATASET profile or segment

          Show dataset profiles that fit all of the following criteria
          Dataset profile . . _____         1 1 EGN mask
          Owned by  . . . . . _____   (group or userid, or filter)   2 Exact
          High level qual . . OMVS____   (qualifier or filter)          3 Match
          Installation data . _____ (substring or *)         4 Any match

          Additional selection criteria
          _  Profile fields    _  Access list    _  Segment presence _  Absence

          Output/run options
          _  Show segments     _  All           _  Enable full ACL   _  Specify scope
          _  Print format         Customize title   Send as e-mail
                Background run      Full detail form  Sort differently    Narrow print
                Print ACL           Resolve to users  Incl operations     Print names
```

Figure 3.37   Searching data set profiles in zSecure

In the list of data set profiles, use **s** to select the one you want to view. Figure 3.38 shows the view of the OMVS.SOW1.HFS profile. This data set contains the hierarchal file system (HFS) that contains the OMVS files.

```
          zSecure Suite DATASET Overview                          Line 1 of 34
          Command ===> _____    Scroll===> PAGE
          starting OMVS                            13 Mar 2006 13:43


          _ Identification                                              DEMO
            Profile name              OMVS.SOW1.HFS
            Type                      GENERIC
            Volume serial list
          _ Effective first qualifier OMVS
          _ Owner                      OMVS____
            Installation data         _____

            User     Access  ACL id   When          Name          InstData
          _ - any -   READ     *      _____  _____
          _ -group-   ALTER  SYSPROG  _____  _____               SYSTEM PRO
          _ STRTASK   UPDATE STRTASK  _____  _____  DIV STARTED TASK USR

            Safeguards                      Other permissions
            Erase on scratch        No      Allow all accesses    WARNING No
            Audit access success/failures U R Universal access authority  NONE
            Global audit success/failures ___  Resource level             0
            User to notify of violation   _____
            Days protection provided #    _____
```

Figure 3.38   Data set profile in zSecure

To modify the profile, overwrite fields and press Enter. You will then get the RACF command that you can modify or execute. Figure 3.39 shows the result of overwriting the profile owner with ORIPOME.

```
                              zSecure Suite - Confirm command
Command ===> _____

Confirm or edit the following command
altdsd 'OMVS.SOW1.HFS' generic  owner(ORIPOME) _____
        _____
        _____
```

Figure 3.39   zSecure shows the RACF command for modifying a profile.

3.6 Additional Information

The manuals document this subject in details. These manuals are particularly relevant:

- *z/OS Security Server RACF Command Language Reference,* which documents the command-line interface for RACF.

- *z/OS Security Server RACF Security Administrator's Guide,* which explains the various resources that RACF can protect.

- IBM LookAt—z/OS Message Help, at http://www-03.ibm.com/servers/eserver/zseries/zos/bkserv/lookat. This search engine has the documentation to interpret all the z/OS messages.

- *z/OS UNIX System Services Planning,* which explains the UNIXPRIV class that protects UNIX System Services.

- *z/OS UNIX Security Fundamentals,* IBM Red Paper, available at www.redbooks.ibm.com/redpapers/pdfs/redp4193.pdf. Appendix A of this document lists BPX profiles that control UNIX functions.

- The UNIX man command for getfacl and setfacl.

- *Multilevel Security and DB2 Row-Level Security Revealed,* IBM Redbook SG24-6480, available at www.ibm.com/redbooks.

CHAPTER 4

Logging

Thus far we have shown how to authenticate users and create profiles that authorize users to use various resources. Now we demonstrate how to log user actions to ensure that users are using their rights appropriately.

Terminology

You will often hear the words *auditing* and *logging* used interchangeably. Don't be confused by the two: Logging is the act of recording information about an event. Auditing is the examination of information, including logs, to ensure compliance with the installation security policy.

Unfortunately, the operating system documentation sometimes uses these terms inconsistently. In the TSO commands, log options are used for logging information about a particular resource, such as when a data set is modified. Audit options are used for logging information about a particular resource's RACF profile, such as when a user is removed from the ACL for a particular resource. ISPF panels just use the term *audit*.

4.1 Configuring Logging

Security log records are stored using the System Management Facility (SMF). This facility also stores other logging records, which are related to availability, hardware reliability, and so on. To configure logging, both SMF and RACF must be configured properly.

Event Logging

SMF is analogous to the Event Log in Windows or syslog in UNIX. Like those subsystems, it contains a large number of events from diverse sources on the operating system. It is more similar to the Event Log than to syslog because the records in SMF are not usable in their raw form and must be unloaded.

4.1.1 SMF Configuration

Before you can audit events using RACF, you need to configure SMF to record the RACF event types. The first step is to identify the current SMF parameters, such as what event types are logged and where. Changing those parameters enables you to change the SMF configuration to add RACF audit records to the records that SMF keeps. To do this, go to SDSF (=S from any ISPF menu) and type **/d smf,o**. This z/OS console command is used to display the full SMF configuration.

Console Commands

When you prefix a command with / in SDSF, it is interpreted as a command to the system console of the mainframe. These commands allow the operator to start, reconfigure, and stop various mainframe subsystems, such as SMF.

For more information about the console, see the *z/OS V1R6.0 MVS System Commands* guide.

After you enter the command, the screen displays the results of the command, as shown in Figure 4.1. The top parameter, MEMBER, is the data set member in one of the parameter library data sets that currently controls SMF configuration.

```
    HQX7708 ----------------  SDSF PRIMARY OPTION MENU  --  39 RESPONSES NOT SHOWN
    COMMAND INPUT ===>                                          SCROLL ===> 1
    RESPONSE=NMP122
     IEE967I 16.39.39 SMF PARAMETERS 685
            MEMBER = SMFPRM00
            MULCFUNC -- DEFAULT
            BUFUSEWARN(25) -- DEFAULT
            BUFSIZMAX(0128M) -- DEFAULT
```

Figure 4.1   The SMF configuration

To see the list of parameter library data sets, run /d parmlib. The result is a list of data sets, ordered by priority, as shown in Figure 4.2.

```
RESPONSE=NMP122
 IEE251I 11.27.15 PARMLIB DISPLAY 759
 PARMLIB DATA SETS SPECIFIED
 AT IPL
 ENTRY  FLAGS  VOLUME  DATA SET
    1      S    R01221  USER.PARMLIB
    2      S    COMN01  COMMON.PARMLIB
    3      D    G1601B  SYS1.PARMLIB
    4      S    G1601B  SYS1.PARMLIB.INSTALL
```

Figure 4.2   The parameter library data sets

Parameter Libraries

The parameter libraries contain operating system parameters. They are roughly equivalent to the /etc directory under UNIX and the Registry under Windows.

One difference is that UNIX and Windows keep only one copy of their configuration. In z/OS, there are multiple copies. For example, Figure 4.2 shows that NMP122 has four configuration data sets. This allows installation to clearly mark which configuration settings are the operating system defaults and which are customized for a particular data center or mainframe. This feature simplifies administration, especially for administers who are new to a particular mainframe. They can easily see what is different from the default.

Another difference is that most parameter "files" (data set members) can have multiple versions. For example, the current SMF parameters are stored in SMFPRM00, as shown in Figure 4.1. However, any other member with the name SMFPRM followed by two characters also contains SMF parameters. This makes it easy to back out of a change when needed and to keep multiple parameter settings when needed.

To find the SMF parameters, look for the SMFPRM00 member in one of the data sets listed. The list is ordered, meaning that the SMFPRM00 in use is the one found in the data set highest in the list. The list of data sets is called the PARMLIB concatenation. Type =3.4 to enter the data set utilities. Type the name of the first data set and click Enter, as shown in Figure 4.3.

```
                        Data Set List Utility
   Option ===> _____
                                                    More:      +
      blank Display data set list          P  Print data set list
          V Display VTOC information        PV Print VTOC information

   Enter one or both of the parameters below:
      Dsname Level . . .  user.parmlib_____
      Volume serial  . .  _____
```

Figure 4.3   Data set utilities

You get a list of matching data sets (in this case, there is only one). Type **B** next to the one you want to browse, as shown in Figure 4.4.

```
DSLIST - Data Sets Matching USER.PARMLIB                              Row 1 of 1
Command ===> _____   Scroll ===> PAGE

Command - Enter "/" to select action              Message          Volume
-------------------------------------------------------------------------------
b       USER.PARMLIB                                                  R01221
****************************** End of Data Set list ******************************
```

Figure 4.4   Selecting a data set

You get a list of members. Type **F <member name from Figure 4.1>** to find the member that has the SMF parameters, as shown in Figure 4.5.

```
BROWSE              USER.PARMLIB                       Row 00001 of 00033
Command ===> f smfprm00_____       Scroll ===> PAGE
          Name     Prompt       Size   Created       Changed          ID
_____  APPCPM00               8    2000/02/14  2000/03/27 13:15:49  LAUFMAN
_____  ASCHPM00               5    2000/02/14  2000/02/14 11:00:46  LAUFMAN
_____  BLSCUSER              65    2003/01/29  2003/01/29 11:59:29  THACKER
_____  BPXPRM01              32    1999/12/21  2003/01/29 12:33:11  THACKER
_____  COMMND01               3    2000/03/29  2005/11/15 17:00:36  JAYHILL
_____  COUPLE01              11    2002/05/03  2005/02/15 08:57:52  LAUFMAN
_____  CTIBB000              50    2003/01/29  2003/01/29 11:36:09  THACKER
```

Figure 4.5   Finding a specific member

If the member is not found, repeat the process with the other parameter libraries in Figure 4.2.

On the system we used for the screenshots, the member SMFPRM00 is in the data set SYS1.PARMLIB.

To configure SMF to support RACF, do the following:

1. Copy the member currently used for SMF configuration to a new member in USER.PARMLIB.

2. Edit the new member to add the RACF event types, and remember the data sets that SMF uses for logging.

3. Use the console command to point SMF to the new configuration.

To copy the member, type **c** next to the member's name, as shown in Figure 4.6.

```
BROWSE              SYS1.PARMLIB                         CHARS 'SMFPRM00' found
Command ===> _____    Scroll ===> PAGE
          Name    Prompt      Size   Created       Changed            ID
c_____ SMFPRM00              15   1999/12/08  2005/04/11 09:21:55  LAUFMAN
_____ TSOKEY00               9   1999/12/08  2000/02/01 16:03:48  LAUFMAN
```

Figure 4.6   Copying the data set with the SMF parameters

In the copy entry panel, type **'USER.PARMLIB'** as the other data set name. The single quotes are necessary because otherwise it will be interpreted as your own personal data set, whose full name is <your user name>.USER.PARMLIB. The new member name must start with SMFPRM, followed by two characters that are unused, to create a new member. Figure 4.7 shows an example, using the name SMFPRMOP. We used Ori's initials to show whose configuration this is; follow any conventions that your site defines for configuration member names.

```
                              COPY Entry Panel
     Command ===> _____
                                                              More:      +
     CURRENT from data set: 'SYS1.PARMLIB(SMFPRM00)'

     To Library                    Options:
         Project . . . _____        Enter "/" to select option
         Group . . . . _____      _  Replace like-named members
         Type  . . . . _____      /  Process member aliases

     To Other Data Set Name
         Data Set Name . . . 'user.parmlib'_____
         Volume Serial . . . _____     (If not cataloged)

     NEW member name  . . . smfprmop  (Blank unless member to be renamed)
```

Figure 4.7   Copy entry panel

After the member is copied, the member list is redisplayed. The word Copied appears next to the member name. However, you will not see the new member even if it is in the same data set.

To refresh the member list, press F3 to exit. You will then be able to type E to edit
USER.PARMLIB again (if you've been editing it) or =3.4 to get back to the data set utilities. Enter
E next to the new member to edit it. Figure 4.8 shows the contents of the new member.

```
 EDIT        USER.PARMLIB(SMFPRMOP)  -  01.00           Columns 00001 00072
 Command ===> _____  Scroll ===> HALF
 ****** **************************** Top of Data *****************************
 ==MSG> -Warning- The UNDO command is not available until you change
 ==MSG>           your edit profile using the command RECOVERY ON.
 000100 ACTIVE
 000200 NOPROMPT
 000300 DSNAME(SYS1.MAN1,SYS1.MAN2,SYS1.MAN3)
 000400 REC(PERM)
 000500 MAXDORM(3000)
 000600 STATUS(010000)
 000700 JWT(2400)
 000800 SID(&SMFID.)
 000900 LISTDSN
 000910 MEMLIMIT(NOLIMIT)
 001000 SYS(TYPE(4,5,6,14,14,26,28,30,37,38,39,64,70,71,72,73,74,75,76,77,78))
 001100 SYS(NODETAIL)
 001200 SYS(NOINTERVAL)
```

Figure 4.8 SMF parameters

Two parameters directly affect RACF auditing. The first, DSNAME, contains the names of
the data sets where SMF writes logging entries. On this system, they are SYS1.MAN1,
SYS1.MAN2, and SYS1.MAN3. The second is SYS(TYPE(x)), which controls the event types that
will be recorded. RACF uses four event types: 30 (common address space work record, which is
also created during job initiation), 80 (resource access), 81 (RACF initialization), and 83 (security event). Make sure these four types are listed in the SMF parameters, and then save the member. If the line becomes too long for the editor (more than 72 characters), end the first line with a
comma and a space, and continue the list of types in the next line (see Figure 4.9).

The other SMF configuration parameters are beyond the scope of this book. If you want to
learn more about this SMF configuration, look in *z/OS V1R6.0 MVS Initialization and Tuning
Reference*, Topic 69.10.

```
 000910 MEMLIMIT(NOLIMIT)
 001000 SYS(TYPE(4,5,6,14,14,26,28,30,37,38,39,64,70,71,72,73,74,75,76,77,78,
 '''''' 80,81,83))
 001100 SYS(NODETAIL)
```

Figure 4.9 Edited SMF parameters for RACF

The new configuration member has been created. The next step is to tell SMF to use the
new configuration member. To do this, return to SDSF and run **/set smf=xx**, where xx is the

two-character ending of the SMFPRMxx data set member you just created. Because the data set member in the example is SMFPRMOP, the command is /set smf=OP (mainframe commands are not case significant). This command returns the names of the data sets that SMF uses for logging, as shown in Figure 4.10.

```
HQX7708 ---------------- SDSF PRIMARY OPTION MENU  -- COMMAND ISSUED
COMMAND INPUT ===>                                       SCROLL ===> 1
RESPONSE=NMP122
 IEE949I 16.58.54 SMF DATA SETS 698
          NAME       VOLSER SIZE(BLKS) %FULL  STATUS
          P-SYS1.MAN1 R01221     7200    16  ACTIVE
          S-SYS1.MAN2 R01221     1800     0  ALTERNATE
          S-SYS1.MAN3 R01221     1800     0  ALTERNATE
 IEE968I NOTIFICATION OF SUBSYS OMVS FAILED -
 IEE968I    SUBSYSTEM DOES NOT EXIST
```

Figure 4.10   SMF parameter member changed

Note

This changes only the configuration used on the running system. To make z/OS use the new SMFPRMxx member after subsequent system restarts, change the SMF= line on the IEASYS00 member in the PARMLIB concatenation, the list of data sets returned by /d parmlib.

Which Member?

When you issue /set smf=OP, the operating system looks for a member called SMF-PRMOP in the PARMLIB concatenation. In most cases, the first parameter library is USER.PARMLIB, which is the reason you put your configuration member there.

To verify that the RACF event types will be logged, enter **/d smf,o** to see the SMF parameters again. The SYS(TYPE(x)) parameter might not be visible onscreen.

To view the complete command output, return to the SDSF menu and type **ULOG** for the user session log, which can be shortened to just **U**. Scroll until you can see the SYS(TYPE(x)) parameter, as shown in Figure 4.11.

```
SDSF ULOG  CONSOLE ORIPOME                          LINE 53      COLUMNS 48- 127
COMMAND INPUT ===> _                                             SCROLL ===> 1
     SYS(NODETAIL) -- PARMLIB
     SYS(TYPE(4,5,6,14,14,26,28,30,37,38,39,64,70,71,72,73,74,75,
     76,77,78,80,81,83)) -- PARMLIB
     MEMLIMIT(NOLIMIT) -- PARMLIB
     LISTDSN -- PARMLIB
```

Figure 4.11   New SYS(TYPE(x)) parameter with the RACF event types

4.1.2 RACF Configuration

At this point, SMF is properly configured to record logging entries from RACF. The next step is to configure RACF to generate the appropriate log entries.

As discussed in the previous chapter, RACF profiles are divided by class, such as DATASET and UNIXPRIV. The log options, which are modified using SETROPTS LOGOPTIONS, control the logging when a resource is used, such as when a data set is opened. The audit options, which are modified using SETR AUDIT, control the logging when the RACF profile for a resource is modified, such as when a user is added to the ACL.

Five possible log settings exist, shown in Table 4.1.

Table 4.1   Log Settings for RACF Classes

Setting	Meaning
Always	Audit all access attempts
Never	Never audit access attempts
Successes	Audit all successful access attempts
Failures	Audit all failed access attempts
Default	Use the audit settings in the profile

To view the RACF options, which include the log settings, from the RACF ISPF menus, type **5.1** at the top RACF menu. Figure 4.12 shows a possible result.

```
LOGOPTIONS "ALWAYS" CLASSES =  NONE
LOGOPTIONS "NEVER" CLASSES =  NONE
LOGOPTIONS "SUCCESSES" CLASSES =  NONE
LOGOPTIONS "FAILURES" CLASSES =  NONE
LOGOPTIONS "DEFAULT" CLASSES =  DATASET ACCTNUM ACICSPCT AIMS ALCSAUTH
                                APPCLU APPCPORT APPCSERV APPCSI APPCTP
                                APPL BCICSPCT CACHECLS CBIND CCICSCMD
                                CDT CIMS CONSOLE CPSMOBJ CPSMXMP CSFKEYS
                                CSFSERV DASDVOL DBNFORM DCEUUIDS DCICSDCT
                                DEVICES DIGTCERT DIGTCRIT DIGTNMAP DIGTRING
                                DIMS DIRACC DIRAUTH DIRECTRY DIRSRCH DLFCLASS
```

Figure 4.12 RACF options (the log options)

Figure 4.12 lists the DATASET class which controls data set logging under default. This lets you control the logging on data set access from the RACF profiles. If it is listed under a different value on your system, you will need to change it. Run this TSO command:

SETROPTS LOGOPTIONS(DEFAULT(dataset))

This command sets the DATASET logging option to default.

The term used in SMF and in the RACF configuration options for tracking system activity is *logging*. The term the ISPF interface uses for the same functionality is *auditing*.

After you configure a class to log based on the profiles of that class, as you have done here with the DATASET class, you can specify logging for specific resources. To do this for data sets, go to the data set menu of RACF. Modify the profile for RACFBK.CNTL, as you learned to do in the previous chapter. Set the audit level for both successes and failures to READ to log every attempt to access (read or higher) the data set, as shown in Figure 4.13.

```
                         RACF - CHANGE DATA SET PROFILE
      COMMAND ===>

         PROFILE: RACFBK.CNTL

      ENTER THE DESIRED CHANGES:
         OWNER                ===>           Userid or group name
         LEVEL                ===>           0-99
         FAILED ACCESSES      ===>           FAIL or WARN
         UACC                 ===>           NONE, READ, UPDATE,
                                             CONTROL, ALTER OR EXECUTE
         AUDIT SUCCESSES      ===> read      READ, UPDATE, CONTROL,
                                             ALTER, or NOAUDIT
         AUDIT FAILURES       ===> read      READ, UPDATE, CONTROL,
                                             ALTER, or NOAUDIT
```

Figure 4.13 Auditing in the profile

Use the editor to open `<username>.RACFBK.CNTL(DSMON)` both as yourself and as MYUSER. Opening the data set as yourself should succeed. Opening it as MYUSER should fail. This generates the audit records you read in the next section.

4.2 Generating Reports

Before you can use the SMF records, you must unload them to a different data set.

4.2.1 Unloading Log Data to Sequential Text Files

To unload the data from SMF to a sequential file, create the following job in `RACFBK.`
`CNTL(AUDIT)` (see Listing 4.1). Wait to submit it until you read the description of the JCL because the `DATE` parameter in the JCL will probably need to be changed. You could just leave out the `DATE` parameter, but depending on the number of SMF records on your system, this could cause the job to run a long time and generate a huge results data set.

Listing 4.1   RACFBK.CNTL(AUDIT)

```
//AUDIT   JOB CLASS=A,NOTIFY=&SYSUID,MSGCLASS=H
//UNLOAD   EXEC PGM=IFASMFDP
//SYSPRINT DD SYSOUT=*
//ADUPRINT DD SYSOUT=*
//OUTDD   DD DSN=&SYSUID..RACF.AUDIT,DISP=(MOD,CATLG,DELETE),
//        UNIT=SYSALLDA,SPACE=(CYL,(10,10)),
//        DCB=(RECFM=VBS,LRECL=8192)
//SMFDATA DD DSN=SYS1.MAN1,DISP=SHR
//SMFOUT   DD DUMMY
//SYSIN   DD *
    INDD(SMFDATA,OPTIONS(DUMP))
    OUTDD(SMFOUT,TYPE(30,80,81,83))
    DATE(2007030,2007090)
    ABEND(NORETRY)
    USER2(IRRADU00)
    USER3(IRRADU86)
```

Here is an explanation of this JCL job:

```
//OUTDD   DD DSN=&SYSUID..RACF.AUDIT,DISP=(MOD,CATLG,DELETE),
//        UNIT=SYSALLDA,SPACE=(CYL,(10,10)),
//        DCB=(RECFM=VBS,LRECL=8192)
```

These lines define the output data set, the one that will contain the log entries.

The data set's name is `&SYSUID..RACF.AUDIT`, which is translated to `<user who ran the job>.RACF.AUDIT`.

When a JCL data definition (DD) uses a data set, the data set disposition is specified in the `DISP` parameter. The first value in this parameter specifies the source of the data set and how it is handled while the program step is running:

- `OLD`—The data set already exists. If it doesn't exist, the job will fail. It will be opened for exclusive access.

- `SHR`—The data set already exists. If it doesn't exist, the job will fail. It will be opened for shared access. This means that other jobs can open the data set for input and read from it while this job runs.

- `MOD`—The data set might or might not already exist. If it does not exist, it will be allocated. This requires the `UNIT` and `SPACE` parameters so that z/OS will know where to allocate it and with what parameters. If it does exist, append to it. Either way, the access is exclusive.

- `NEW`—The data set does not exist. It is allocated and opened for exclusive access. This requires the `UNIT` and `SPACE` parameters. If the data set already exists, the job will fail.

The second and third parameters tell z/OS what to do with the data set when the program step ends. The second parameter applies when the program step completes successfully or if there is no third parameter. The third parameter, if used, applies in case the program step fails. These are the possible values:

- `KEEP`—Keep the data set without any changes to the Storage Management Subsystem (SMS) catalog.

- `CATLG`—Keep the data set and add it to an SMS catalog.

- `UNCATLG`—Keep the data set, but remove it from the catalog.

- `PASS`—Keep the data set for another step in the same job. This lets the output of one program become the input of the next one, similar to pipes in a UNIX environment.

- `DELETE`—Delete the data set.

`UNIT=SYSALLDA` specifies that if the data set is created, it can be created on any disk drive. `SPACE=(CYL,(10,10))` specifies the storage for the new data set, if it is created. This value means that the first extent of the data set will be ten disk cylinders and that each additional extent will also be ten disk cylinders. Because a data set can have up to 16 extents, this means the total data set size will never exceed 160 cylinders.

The final parameter is `DCB=(RECFM=VBS,LRECL=8192)`. If the DD statement creates a new data set, this parameter defines the data control block for the new data set. In contrast to UNIX and Windows, which treat files as streams of bytes, the mainframe keeps information about the structure of the data set as a set of records.

The first parameter inside the data control block (DCB) is RECFM, which defines the record format. VBS stands for variable-length records, blocked, and spanned. *Variable* means that the record length varies. *Blocked* means that each data set block can include multiple records. In unblocked access, each record corresponds to a single block, which is inefficient use of disk space for small records. *Spanned* means that a record can be divided between two blocks, if necessary. To learn more about data set record formats, see *z/OS DFSMS Using Data Sets* in the library center.

The second parameter in DCB is LRECL. For fixed-length records, LRECL specifies the record length. For variable-length records, such as here, LRECL specifies the maximum length. In this case, the maximum record length is set to 8,192 bytes.

```
//SMFDATA DD DSN=SYS1.MAN1,DISP=SHR
```

This line defines the log record data set that will be used as input for the job. The name of the data set is taken from the SMF parameters, as seen with an ACTIVE status in Figure 4.10. The disposition is shared, meaning that other tasks can use the same data set at the same time.

```
//SMFOUT   DD DUMMY
```

This line defines SMFOUT as a dummy. IFASMFDP, the utility that translates SMF records to sequential text files, also has capabilities to filter SMF records and copy them to a new data set. This line disables this functionality:

```
//SYSIN   DD *
```

SYSIN contains the control statements for IFASMFDP. This line specifies that the data for SYSIN will follow in the JCL job. We explain the configuration options used in the job here, but to learn more about the configuration options available with IFASMFDP, see *z/OS V1R6.0 MVS System Management Facility (SMF)*, Topic 3.1.1, "Processing the SMF Dump Program."

```
INDD(SMFDATA,OPTIONS(DUMP))
```

This line specifies that the input will be the SMFDATA data definition, defined earlier as: SYS1.MAN1. DUMP specifies that the records will be read but not modified (the other options are CLEAR—delete the records in the data set—and ALL—read the records and then delete them). The TYPE parameter specifies which SMF types to unload—in this case, we are interested in only those that are relevant to RACF: 30, 80, 81, and 83.

```
OUTDD(SMFOUT,TYPE(30,80,81,83))
```

IFASMFDP copies the records into an output data set specified by the OUTDD statement. SMFOUT was defined earlier as a dummy, so it does nothing.

```
DATE(2007030,2007090)
```

This line specifies the start and end dates. The mainframe date format is the year followed by the number of the day in the year. This date format, specified in ISO-8601, is sometimes called the Julian date. This line specifies records from the thirtieth day of 2007 (January 30) until the

ninetieth day (March 31). These values were useful when this chapter was written; when you run
the job on your own system, change them to the desired interval.

Converting Dates

One way to convert between this format and regular dates is with a tool that does date arith-
metic, such as Microsoft® Excel. The day number is the difference in days between a date and
December 31 on the previous year.

Another way is to use the online calendar calculator at www.fourmilab.ch/documents/calendar.

```
ABEND(NORETRY)
```

Abend is a mainframe term that is analogous to *crash*. *Abend* is short for "abnormal end." If
the program abends, this line specifies that the system should not try to rerun it.

```
USER2(IRRADU00)
USER3(IRRADU86)
```

These lines specify common exit routines (mainframe term for hooks) that RACF uses to
process RACF SMF records.

Now, modify the DATE parameter to a value appropriate for when you are reading this and
submit the job.

This job should create a data set called <USERID>.RACF.AUDIT, which contains the SMF
log records.

4.2.2 Understanding Sequential Reports

Browse the RACF.AUDIT data set created in the previous section. Type the command COLS ON to
view the column numbers. It shows the tens digit of the column number above the text.

Figure 4.14 shows part of a RACF.AUDIT data set.

```
   BROWSE     ORIPOME.RACF.AUDIT                   Line 00000196 Col 001 080
   Command ===> _____  Scroll ===> 1____
   ----+----1----+----2----+----3----+----4----+----5----+----6----+----7----+----8
   JOBINIT   TERM      16:14:19 2007-02-20 IP01             ORIPOME  OMVS
   SETROPTS  SUCCESS   17:04:24 2007-02-20 IP01 NO    NO   NO   ORIPOME  OMVS      NO
   ALTDSD    SUCCESS   17:12:18 2007-02-20 IP01 NO    NO   NO   ORIPOME  OMVS      NO
   ACCESS    SUCCESS   17:12:24 2007-02-20 IP01 NO    NO   NO   ORIPOME  OMVS      YES
   ACCESS    SUCCESS   17:15:28 2007-02-20 IP01 NO    NO   NO   ORIPOME  OMVS      YES
```

Figure 4.14 Auditing results

Each line in this data set is a separate record. The format of the unloaded SMF records is
documented in *z/OS Security Server RACF Macros and Interfaces,* Chapter 6. For example, let's

review the bottom line shown in Figure 4.14, the one for an access request at 17:15:28 on February 20, 2007.

The first fields are the same for all records of types 30 and 80. These fields are documented in Topic 6.2, "The Format of the Header Portion of the Unloaded SMF Records." For every field, this topic contains the field name and an explanation, as well as the start and end columns for the field. For example, the event type starts at position 1 and ends in position 8. The event qualifier starts at position 10 and ends at position 17. Therefore, the event type is ACCESS and the qualifier is SUCCESS.

The job name is at positions 180–187. To see that portion of the record, press F11 to scroll right until you reach column 161, as shown in Figure 4.15. Because the first column is 161, as shown in the upper-right corner of the screen, the 8 on the columns line stands for column 180. Therefore, the job name is ORIPOME, the TSO login for the user ORIPOME.

```
   BROWSE     ORIPOME.RACF.AUDIT                          Line 00000196 Col 161 240
   Command ===> _____ Scroll ===> 1___
   ----+----7----+----8----+----9----+----0----+----1----+----2----+----3----+----4
                     DSMON     16:14:18 2007-02-20
   NO   NO   NT73L701 ORIPOME  16:12:41 2007-02-20        NO    NO    NO    NO    NO
   NO   NO   NT73L701 ORIPOME  16:12:41 2007-02-20        NO    NO    NO    NO    NO
   NO   NO   NT73L701 ORIPOME  16:12:41 2007-02-20        NO    NO    NO    NO    NO
   NO   NO   NT73L701 ORIPOME  16:12:41 2007-02-20        NO    NO    NO    NO    NO
```

Figure 4.15   The job name

Topic 6.2, "The Format of the Header Portion," describes only the header information, which is common to most records. To see the extensions specific to event types, see Topic 6.3, "Event Codes." According to that topic, lines with the ACCESS event type describe access to resources that are not (UNIX System Services) files or directories, and those lines are further documented in Topic 6.4.3 (for z/OS Version 1.6—other versions might have it in a different topic). That topic lists the fields in the record. The next topic, Topic 6.4.4, lists the event qualifiers. Because the event qualifier is SUCCESS, Topic 6.4.4 tells you that the record describes a successful access attempt.

According to Topic 6.4.3, the name of the resource requested starts at position 282. Therefore, as Figure 4.16 shows, this record refers to access of ORIPOME.RACFBK.CNTL. The level of access requested is in positions 538–545, the level of access granted is in 547–554, and so on. RACF log records provide a lot of information about who attempted to do what on the z/OS system.

```
   BROWSE     ORIPOME.RACF.AUDIT                          Line 00000196 Col 241 320
   Command ===> _____ Scroll ===> PAGE
   ----+----5----+----6----+----7----+----8----+----9----+----0----+----1----+----2
   NO   NO   NO   NO   NO        7709 ORIPOME              NO   NO   NO   NO
   NO   NO   NO   NO   NO        7709 ORIPOME  ORIPOME
   NO   NO   NO   NO   NO        7709 ORIPOME.RACFBK.CNTL
   NO   NO   NO   NO   NO        7709 ORIPOME.RACFBK.CNTL
```

Figure 4.16   The resource accessed

4.2.3 Generating Reports with ICETOOL

> **Note**
>
> This section uses DFSORT™, which is a separately licensed program. It is very common on z/OS systems, and your mainframe might have it. If it does not, you probably have some competing sort package to generate reports, such as SYNCSORT. Ask a system programmer for help.

The format of the data unloaded from SMF is not very user friendly. It contains all the records from the report period rather than just the relevant ones. You might have to consult the documentation to interpret what each field means.

ICETOOL, which is part of DFSORT, allows for more user-friendly reports. To use it, copy the batch job `RACFBK.CNTL(AUDIT)` to `RACFBK.CNTL(REPORT)` (the method to copy data set members is covered in Section 4.1.1, "SMF Configuration"). Then modify the file as shown in the bolded lines of Listing 4.2 and submit the job.

Listing 4.2   RACFBK.CNTL(REPORT)

```
//REPORT   JOB CLASS=A,NOTIFY=&SYSUID,MSGCLASS=H
//UNLOAD   EXEC PGM=IFASMFDP
//SYSPRINT DD SYSOUT=*
//ADUPRINT DD SYSOUT=*
//OUTDD    DD DSN=&&RECS,DISP=(MOD,PASS,DELETE),
//         UNIT=SYSALLDA,SPACE=(CYL,(10,10)),
//         DCB=(RECFM=VBS,LRECL=8192)
//SMFDATA DD DSN=SYS1.MAN1,DISP=SHR
//SMFOUT   DD DUMMY
//SYSIN   DD *
    INDD(SMFDATA,OPTIONS(DUMP))
    OUTDD(SMFOUT,TYPE(30,80,81,83))
    DATE(2007030,2007090)
    ABEND(NORETRY)
    USER2(IRRADU00)
    USER3(IRRADU86)
```

```
//DELOLD  EXEC PGM=IEFBR14 Delete old report
//DELME   DD DSN=&SYSUID..REPORT.TEXT,DISP=(MOD,DELETE,DELETE),
//        UNIT=SYSALLDA,SPACE=(CYL,(1,1))
//GENRPRT EXEC PGM=ICETOOL Generate the report
//TOOLMSG DD SYSOUT=*
//DFSMSG  DD SYSOUT=*
//TOOLIN  DD *
  SORT FROM(RECS) TO(SORTED) USING(USER)
  DISPLAY FROM(SORTED) LIST(REPORT) DATE TITLE('Resource Access') -
     BTITLE('User:') BREAK(63,8,CH) -
     HEADER('Viol') ON(48,4,CH) -
     HEADER('Date') ON(32,10,CH) -
     HEADER('Time') ON(23,8,CH) -
     HEADER('Resource') ON(286,30,CH) -
     HEADER('Result') ON(14,8,CH) -
     BLANK
//RECS     DD DSN=&&RECS,DISP=(OLD,DELETE)
//REPORT   DD DSN=&SYSUID..REPORT.TEXT,DISP=(NEW,CATLG,DELETE),
//            UNIT=SYSALLDA,SPACE=(CYL,(1,1)),
//            DCB=(RECFM=FB,LRECL=80)
//SORTED   DD DSN=&&SORT,DISP=(NEW,DELETE)
//USERCNTL DD *
     SORT FIELDS=(63,8,CH,A)
     INCLUDE COND=(5,6,CH,EQ,C'ACCESS')
```

> **Note**
>
> In the interest of simplicity, this job unloads the SMF records and then generates a report. On production systems with heavy logging loads, that would be tremendously wasteful. Instead, you would write one job to unload the SMF records to a data set and other jobs that produce reports.

The resulting output is placed in REPORT.TEXT. It should look similar to Figure 4.17.

```
  BROWSE     ORIPOME.REPORT.TEXT                    Line 00000000 Col 001 080
  Command ===> _____ Scroll ===> PAGE
  ******************************** Top of Data *********************************
  02/22/07         RESOURCE ACCESS

  USER:  MYUSER

  VIOL   DATE         TIME      RESOURCE                       RESULT
  ----   ----------   --------  ------------------------------ --------
  NO     2007-02-22   23:08:59  ORIPOME.RACFBK.CNTL            SUCCESS
  YES    2007-02-22   23:09:04  ORIPOME.RACFBK.CNTL            INSAUTH
  02/22/07         RESOURCE ACCESS

  USER:  ORIPOME

  VIOL   DATE         TIME      RESOURCE                       RESULT
  ----   ----------   --------  ------------------------------ --------
  NO     2007-02-20   17:12:24  ORIPOME.RACFBK.CNTL            SUCCESS
  NO     2007-02-20   17:15:28  ORIPOME.RACFBK.CNTL            SUCCESS
  NO     2007-02-20   17:18:33  ORIPOME.RACFBK.CNTL            SUCCESS
```

Figure 4.17   Report from the audit data

How does it work? The first execution step of the JCL, which unloads data from SMF, is almost identical to RACFBK.CNTL(AUDIT). The only difference is in the OUTDD data definition:

```
//OUTDD    DD DSN=&&RECS,DISP=(MOD,PASS,DELETE),
//         UNIT=SYSALLDA,SPACE=(CYL,(10,10)),
//         DCB=(RECFM=VBS,LRECL=8192)
```

The data set name here is &&RECS. When a data set name in JCL starts with two ampersands, it means that it is a temporary data set, for use only in this job. The operating system names it because the name is not important. The PASS in the disposition specifies that the data stream will be passed to an execution step later in the job. The DELETE specifies if this execution step fails—and, therefore, the job stops—the temporary data set can be deleted.

Because the unloaded SMF data will be used only for creating the report, there is no need to keep it afterward.

```
//DELOLD   EXEC PGM=IEFBR14 Delete old report
//DELME    DD DSN=&SYSUID..REPORT.TEXT,DISP=(MOD,DELETE,DELETE),
//         UNIT=SYSALLDA,SPACE=(CYL,(1,1))
```

The second execution step deletes the old report, if one exists. It runs IEFBR14, which is a dummy program that does nothing. The DELME DD statement for this step specifies MOD on &SYSUID..REPORT.TEXT, so the program will be able to open the data set whether or not it exists. Then, when the program is done, it will delete the data set.

```
//GENRPRT EXEC PGM=ICETOOL Generate the report
```

The last execution step calls a program named ICETOOL, which is used to manipulate data and generate reports in a mainframe environment. It is a programmer-friendly front end to the DFSORT data-manipulation utilities. For a complete description of ICETOOL, see Chapter 6 in *z/OS V1R6.0 DFSORT Application Programming Guide*.

```
//TOOLIN  DD *
```

TOOLIN is the data stream that controls ICETOOL. Each operator in TOOLIN can be one line or more. If an operator spans more than a single line, each line but the last must end with a hyphen as a continuation symbol.

```
SORT FROM(RECS) TO(SORTED) USING(USER)
```

This operator specifies that ICETOOL will take the records from RECS, sort and select them according to the rules in the USERCNTL data stream, and output them to SORTED—all defined using DD in this execution step. ICETOOL does not allow the sorting rules to be specified directly in TOOLIN; they must be specified in a separate data stream. The USING(xxxx) clause always appends CNTL to the USING(xxx) value to get the name of the data stream, resulting in USERCNTL.

Because we use it here, let's jump ahead to the definition of USERCNTL.

```
//USERCNTL DD *
    SORT FIELDS=(63,8,CH,A)
    INCLUDE COND=(5,6,CH,EQ,C'ACCESS')
```

This data definition has two parts: a sort rule and a select rule.

```
    SORT FIELDS=(63,8,CH,A)
```

For reasons that will be explained later, the records need to be sorted by user ID. This line specifies the sort fields. In this case, there is one field, which starts in byte 63 of the record and continues for 8 bytes. It is a character field, and the sort order is ascending.

According to the documentation (Topic 6.2 in *z/OS V1R6.0 Security Server RACF Macros and Interfaces*), the user name field starts at byte 59. However, because the data set uses variable-size records, each record starts with a 4-byte record length. For that reason, we need to add 4 to the starting location for every field.

```
    INCLUDE COND=(5,6,CH,EQ,C'ACCESS')
```

This line requires the six characters starting in location 5, which is location 1 in the table, to be equal to the character string ACCESS. This limits the results to resource access records.

Using the full definition of USERCNTL, SORTED will have the resource access records and they will be sorted by user.

```
DISPLAY FROM(SORTED) LIST(REPORT) DATE TITLE('Resource Access') -
```

This line directs ICETOOL to create a report from the records in SORTED and write it to REPORT. This line also specifies that the top line of each report page must include the date the report was created and the title `Resource Access`. The hyphen sign at the end of the line speci-fies that the next line is a continuation.

```
BTITLE('User:') BREAK(63,8,CH) -
```

This line specifies that the report is broken up by the character field that starts at byte 63 and continues for 8 bytes (the user field). Every time a new user name is encountered, the report will write `User:` followed by the user name. This division into sections is the reason the records had to be sorted by user name earlier.

```
HEADER('Viol') ON(48,4,CH) -
HEADER('Date') ON(32,10,CH) -
HEADER('Time') ON(23,8,CH) -
HEADER('Resource') ON(286,30,CH) -
HEADER('Result') ON(14,8,CH) -
```

These lines specify the columns in the report. The `HEADER` specifies the name that will be displayed, and the `ON` specifies the first byte, the length, and the format. Because the unloaded records already use characters, the format is always `CH`.

```
BLANK
```

This line specifies that columns for character fields must be as narrow as possible while fit-ting their header and the length of their data. Without it, all character columns would be at least 20 characters wide and this report would be wider than a single screen.

ICETOOL retrieves different fields from data streams, sorts them, and rewrites them in a different format. This is similar to the functionality provided by `sort`, `cut`, and `awk` in UNIX.

4.2.4 Other Types of Reports

In addition to ICETOOL, the SMF records can be unloaded to a DB2 database if you have DB2 on your system. This is explained in Topic 3.6 of *z/OS V1R7.0 Security Server RACF Auditor's Guide*.

Starting with z/OS Version 1.7, it is also possible to unload the SMF data as XML. To do that, use the same job as in Listing 4.1, but specify `XMLOUT` instead of `OUTDD` in the data definition.

At this point, you know how to perform the basics of computer security with RACF: authen-ticate users, authorize them to access resources, and log their activities. The following chapter teaches you the basics of auditing and how to verify that a mainframe is configured to be secure.

4.3 UNIX System Services (USS) Logging

Three steps are involved in logging information from USS:

1. Ensure that the relevant classes are active.

2. Modify the SMF settings.

3. Specify logging on specific files and directories.

4. Create reports based on the SMF logs.

For more information about USS logging, see the *z/OS UNIX System Services Planning Guide,* Chapter 19, "Monitoring the z/OS UNIX Environment."

4.3.1 Classes for USS Logging

These classes define auditing for various actions in USS:

- DIRACC—Read and write requests on USS files and directories

- DIRSRCH—Directory searches

- FSOBJ—File system requests that aren't included in DIRACC and DIRSRCH

- FSSEC—Changes to the security data of files and directories

- IPCOBJ—Interprocess communication

- PROCACT—Actions that affect processes, such as ps and nice

- PROCESS—Changes to the UID and GID of processes

To verify that these classes are set to default logging, issue this TSO command:

SETROPTS LIST

See that they are listed under LOGOPTIONS "DEFAULT," as Figure 4.18 shows for DIRACC.

```
LOGOPTIONS "FAILURES" CLASSES =  NONE
LOGOPTIONS "DEFAULT" CLASSES =  DATASET ACCTNUM ACICSPCT AIMS ALCSAUTH
                                APPCLU APPCPORT APPCSERV APPCSI APPCTP
                                APPL BCICSPCT CACHECLS CBIND CCICSCMD
                                CDT CIMS CONSOLE CPSMOBJ CPSMXMP CSFKEYS
                                CSFSERV DASDVOL DBNFORM DCEUUIDS DCICSDCT
                                DEVICES DIGTCERT DIGTCRIT DIGTNMAP DIGTRING
                                DIRACC DIRAUTH DIRECTRY DIRSRCH DLFCLASS
```

Figure 4.18   DIRACC is set to default logging

If those classes are not set to default, run these commands to set them.

```
SETROPTS LOGOPTIONS(DEFAULT(DIRACC))
SETROPTS LOGOPTIONS(DEFAULT(DIRSRCH))
SETROPTS LOGOPTIONS(DEFAULT(FSOBJ))
SETROPTS LOGOPTIONS(DEFAULT(FSSEC))
SETROPTS LOGOPTIONS(DEFAULT(IPCOBJ))
SETROPTS LOGOPTIONS(DEFAULT(PROCACT))
SETROPTS LOGOPTIONS(DEFAULT(PROCESS))
```

4.3.2 SMF Settings for USS

USS can have different SMF settings from the rest of z/OS. To activate security auditing on USS, add this line to the parameter data set member you edited in Section 4.1.1, "SMF Configuration." Either add these lines or modify SUBSYS(OMVS,TYPE(...)) if it already exists.

```
SUBSYS(OMVS,TYPE(4,5,6,14,14,26,28,30,37,38,39,64,70,71,72,73,
74,75,76,77,78,80,81,83))
```

Then go to SDSF (=S) and enter the console commands to reread the parameter data set member and then display the SMF setting. If your member's name is SMFPRMOP, these are the commands:

```
/set smf=op
/d smf,o
```

The parameters should include the parameters for USS, as shown in Figure 4.19. Note that type 80 is shown in the SUBSYS(OMVS,TYPE(...)) line, as shown by the arrow.

```
HQX7708 ---------------- SDSF PRIMARY OPTION MENU  --  39 RESPONSES NOT SHOWN
COMMAND INPUT ===>  _                                     SCROLL ===>  1
RESPONSE=NMP122
 IEE967I 21.48.44 SMF PARAMETERS 539
         MEMBER = SMFPRMOP
         MULCFUNC -- DEFAULT
         BUFUSEWARN(25) -- DEFAULT
         BUFSIZMAX(0128M) -- DEFAULT
         DDCONS(YES) -- DEFAULT
         LASTDS(MSG) -- DEFAULT
         NOBUFFS(MSG) -- DEFAULT
         SYNCVAL(00) -- DEFAULT
         INTVAL(30) -- DEFAULT
         DUMPABND(RETRY) -- DEFAULT
         SUBSYS(OMVS,NODETAIL) -- SYS
         SUBSYS(OMVS,NOINTERVAL) -- SYS
         SUBSYS(OMVS,TYPE(4,5,6,14,14,26,28,30,37,38,39,64,70,71,72,73,
         74,75,76,77,78,80,81,83)) -- PARMLIB
         SUBSYS(OMVS,EXITS(IEFU83)) -- PARMLIB
         SUBSYS(OMVS,EXITS(IEFUJI)) -- PARMLIB
```

Figure 4.19   SMF parameters with USS logging

4.3.3 Specifying Logging in USS

To specify logging for actions on a file or directory, enter OMVS and use the chaudit command. To view the audit settings, use ls -W.

It is possible to audit any of the three UNIX file actions: read (r), write (w), and execute (x). These actions can be audited when permission is granted so the request is successful (s), when permission is not granted and request fails (f), or in all cases (a).

The first format for chaudit is to specify the actions, an equal sign (=), and the conditions under which they will be audited. For example, the following command specifies that any attempt to read or write `acl_test`, whether or not it is successful, will be audited. This format deletes any previous audit settings.

```
chaudit rw=sf acl_test
```

The second format is to specify the actions, a plus sign (+), and then the conditions. This adds auditing on a particular action. For example, to log failed attempts to execute `acl_test`, run this:

```
chaudit x+f acl_test
```

The third format is to specify the actions, a minus sign (−), and then the conditions. This removes auditing on a particular action. For example, to avoid logging failed reads on `acl_test`, run this:

```
chaudit r-f acl_test
```

Now view the audit settings:

```
ls -W acl_test
```

They should be the same as in Figure 4.20.

```
ORIPOME:/u/oripome>chaudit rw=sf acl_test
ORIPOME:/u/oripome>chaudit x+f acl_test
ORIPOME:/u/oripome>chaudit r-f acl_test
ORIPOME:/u/oripome>ls -W acl_test
-rw-r-----+ saf---  1 ORIPOME  CBCFG1        0 Jul 30 08:53 acl_test
ORIPOME:/u/oripome>
```

Figure 4.20   Audit settings on a USS file

Auditor Audit Settings

In Figure 4.20, three other characters come after the ones for the audit settings you just created. These are for the audit settings for auditors, users with special permissions that are explained in Chapter 6, "Limited-Authority RACF Administrators."

Neither the owner of a file nor the UNIX system administrators can modify these permissions. Having these audit bits makes it harder for users to hide their actions, which helps keep people honest.

Now try to write to the file, read from it, and execute it. The first two should succeed, and the last fail:

```
ls -W acl_test >> acl_test
cat acl_test
./acl_test
```

4.3.4 Viewing the USS Log Records

Going back to *z/OS Security Server RACF Macros and Interfaces,* Topic 6.3, "Event Codes," you can see that the event code for checking access to a file is FACCESS. Looking at Table 61 for the details, the user name is in positions 291–310 and the path name is in positions 572–1594. If the requested access was read, it would be in positions 1651–1654, write in 1656–1659, and execute in 1661–1664.

Run the RACFBK.CNTL(AUDIT) job again. When it is done, open RACF.AUDIT and use the command F FACCESS to find the relevant lines. Scroll to the right (F11) to see the other fields.

Modifying RACFBK.CNTL(REPORT) to produce a report of file access in USS is left as an exercise to the student.

4.4 Logging in zSecure

zSecure Audit handles the SMF formats for you. To access SMF, add the SMF data sets to the zSecure input files, as shown in Figure 4.21.

```
                        zSecure Suite - Setup - Input files     Row 2 from 2
    Command ===> _____ Scroll ===> CSR

    Description . . . . SMF Log
    Complex . . . . . . _____
    RRSF node . . . . . _____      Local node for RRSF

    Enter data set names and types.       Type END or press F3 when complete.
    Enter dsname with .* to get a list    Type SAVE to save set, CANCEL to quit.
    Valid line commands: E I R D          Type REFRESH to submit unload  job.

      Data set or Unix file name                          Type      NJE node
    _  'SYS1.MAN1'                                         SMF_      _____
```

Figure 4.21   Adding SMF to the zSecure input files

The events menu lets you decide which type of log entries you want to see, as shown in Figure 4.22.

```
                           zSecure Suite - Main menu
        Option ===> _
                                                                More:      +
        SE   Setup              Options and input data sets

        RA   RACF               RACF Administration

        AA   ACF2               ACF2 Administration

        AU   Audit              Audit security and system resources

        EV   Events             Event reporting from SMF and other logs
          U    User               User events from SMF
          G    Group              Group events from SMF
          D    Data set           Data set events from SMF
          R    Resource           General resource events from SMF
          F    Filesystem         Unix filesystem events from SMF and other logs
          I    IP                 IP events from SMF and other logs
          T    TSS                TSS logging for specific events
          1    SMF reports        Predefined analysis reports
          2    RACF events        RACF logging for specific events
```

Figure 4.22   The zSecure event menu

Next, you specify a filter for the events you want. Figure 4.23 shows a possible filter for data set events.

```
                       zSecure Suite - Events - Data set Selection
        Command ===> _____  _ start panel

        Show records that fit all of the following criteria:
        Data set name . . . *.PARMLIB_____
        System  . . . . . . ____         (system name or EGN mask)

        Advanced selection criteria
        _  Date and time          _  Further data set selection

        Output/run options
        _  Include detail         _  Summarize           _  Specify scope
        _  Output in print format    Customize title        Send as e-mail
             Run in background       Sort differently
```

Figure 4.23   zSecure filter for data set events

After you do this, zSecure displays the list of relevant SMF records, such as those shown in Figure 4.24.

```
IBM Tivoli zSecure SMF display                              Line 1 of 12
Command ===>                                              Scroll===> 1
SMF records for data sets like *.PARMLIB      22Aug07 13:37 to 22Aug07 15:20
me       Description
:37:42.61 RACF ACCESS success for RDUBERT: (READ,READ) on DATASET SYS1.PARMLIB
:37:42.61 RACF ACCESS success for RDUBERT: (READ,READ) on DATASET SYS1.PARMLIB
:37:47.80 RACF ACCESS success for RDUBERT: (READ,READ) on DATASET SYS1.PARMLIB
:37:49.43 RACF ACCESS success for RDUBERT: (READ,READ) on DATASET SYS1.PARMLIB
:04:00.80 RACF ACCESS success for RDUBERT: (READ,READ) on DATASET SYS1.PARMLIB
:04:00.80 RACF ACCESS success for RDUBERT: (READ,READ) on DATASET SYS1.PARMLIB
:04:15.80 RACF ACCESS success for RDUBERT: (READ,READ) on DATASET SYS1.PARMLIB
:19:29.63 RACF ACCESS violation for RESOLVER: (READ,NONE) on DATASET SYS1.PARML
:19:31.94 RACF ACCESS success for STRTASK: (READ,READ) on DATASET SYS1.PARMLIB
:20:04.46 RACF PERMIT success for RDUBERT: PERMIT DATASET SYSS.PARMLIB
:20:04.68 RACF PERMIT success for RDUBERT: PERMIT DATASET SYS1.PARMLIB
:20:56.76 RACF PERMIT success for RDUBERT: PERMIT DATASET SYS1.PARMLIB
******************************** Bottom of Data ********************************
```

Figure 4.24   zSecure displays SMF events.

4.5 Additional Information

The manuals document this subject in details. These manuals are particularly relevant:

- *z/OS MVS System Commands,* which explains console commands

- *z/OS MVS Initialization and Tuning Reference,* which explains how to tune SMF parameters, such as the parameters that control RACF auditing

- *z/OS DFSMS Using Data Sets,* which explains the parameters used to create data sets, including when creating them in JCL

- *z/OS MVS System Management Facility (SMF),* which explains how to dump SMF records into a data set

- *z/OS Security Server RACF Macros and Interfaces,* which documents the format of RACF SMF records

- *z/OS DFSORT Getting Started,* which introduces ICETOOL and the other DFSORT utilities

- *z/OS DFSORT Application Programming Guide,* which includes a detailed explanation on how to use ICETOOL to create reports

- *z/OS UNIX System Services Planning,* which explains USS logging

Auditing

Few things instill more fear in security administrators and systems programmers than learning that their system has been selected for an audit. That's really a shame because when a system is properly managed, having an auditor review the system should result in the auditor finding nothing significant. The best way to ensure that is to routinely review your system and fix problems before the auditor comes to town. In this chapter, we introduce you to the role of the auditor and show the various RACF utilities you can use to help ensure that your system passes muster.

5.1 Auditing

At a high level, the auditor has a very simple job: ensure that the installation security policy is being followed. The auditor might want to look at lots of things, many of which are outside the scope of this book. For example, the auditor might look at the physical controls on your data center, your hiring policies for your systems staff, and your change-control policies and practices.

For the z/OS portion of the audit, the items of interest to your auditor can be divided into two broad categories:

- Static system configuration information, such as which user IDs are defined with system level authorities.

- Dynamic event information that is generated during the normal operation of the system, such as log records that are created when resources are accessed

In Chapter 4, "Logging," you learned how to capture event information for an audit. In this chapter, you learn how to display the system configuration to show an auditor that it is configured correctly.

You can use several RACF functions to review your system's configuration:

- The RACF Data Security Monitor (DSMON), which examines key system settings
- The RACF options, available using the `SETROPTS` command
- The RACF Data Base Unload Utility (IRRDBU00), which unloads your RACF database into a format that can be easily fed into your favorite reporting tools
- The RACF Remove ID Utility, which finds "residual" authorities on your system
- The RACF health checks that are a part of the IBM Health Checker for z/OS

The following sections look at each of these and show how they can be a part of the audit process.

5.2 The RACF Data Security Monitor (DSMON)

The RACF Data Security Monitor (DSMON) utility provides an overview of the security settings on your z/OS system. DSMON creates several different reports on the security characteristics of your system. You can either ask for each report individually or ask for DSMON to create a default set.

Table 5.1 shows the different reports created by DSMON. The most important reports are explained later in this section. For information about the other reports, refer to *z/OS Security Server RACF Auditor's Guide.*

Table 5.1   DSMON Reports

Report Name	Description
SYSTEM	Overall information about the z/OS environment.
RACGRP	The Group Tree Report, which shows the group structure for the entire system.
SYSPPT	Program Properties Table Report, which shows the programs that run with extraordinary authority.
RACAUT	RACF Authorized Caller Table Report, which shows the unauthorized programs that are allowed to use the `RACROUTE  REQUEST=LIST` and `RACROUTE REQUEST=VERIFY` functions.
RACCDT	RACF Class Descriptor Table Report, which shows the general resource classes defined on the system.
RACEXT	RACF Exits Report, which shows the RACF exits being used.
RACGAC	RACF Global Access Table Report, which shows the entries in the RACF Global Access Table.

Report Name	Description
RACSPT	RACF Started Procedure Table Report, which shows the assignments of identities to started procedures.
RACUSR	User Attribute Report, which shows the attributes for users.
SYSLNK, SYSAPF, SYSCAT, RACDST, and SYSSDS	These are the various data sets that can appear in the Selected Data Set Report. Each represents data sets that have a key impact on your z/OS environment. These data sets are in each report: • Link list data sets (SYSLNK) • Authorized program facility (APF) data sets (SYSAPF) • Catalogs (SYSCAT) • Data sets that comprise the RACF database (RACDST) • Other system data sets (SYSSDS)
USRDSN	Installation-specified data set names

5.2.1 Running DSMON

DSMON is typically run as a batch job. Listing 5.1 shows the JCL to run DSMON with the "default" set of reports (which are the SYSAPF, SYSLNK, SYSSDS, SYSCAT, SYSPPT, RACAUT, RACEXT, RACDST, RACUSR, RACSPT, RACCDT, RACGAC, and RACGRP reports).

Listing 5.1   JCL Job to Run DSMON

```
//DSMON     JOB   CLASS=A,NOTIFY=&SYSUID,MSGCLASS=H
//DSMON     EXEC  PGM=ICHDSM00
//SYSPRINT  DD    SYSOUT=*
//SYSUT2    DD    SYSOUT=*
//SYSIN     DD    DUMMY
```

You can run this job by placing this JCL into your data set RACFBK.CNTL(DSMON). Save and submit the job, just as you submitted batch jobs in the earlier chapters.

```
//SYSPRINT  DD    SYSOUT=*
//SYSUT2    DD    SYSOUT=*
```

These lines tell the job entry subsystem to place the output in the same place where the job messages are directed, which, in this case, is also the held queue.

You can now use SDSF to browse the output of the DSMON utility. To do this, go into SDSF (**=s**). From the SDSF primary option panel, select **H** or **O**. SDSF displays a list of the jobs that have held output. (If no jobs are listed, enter the **PREFIX DSMON*** command to tell SDSF to

retrieve output from any job that has a name that begins with DSMON). From that list, select the job
that you just submitted by placing an **s** in the NP column, as shown in Figure 5.1.

```
       SDSF OUTPUT ALL CLASSES ALL FORMS      LINES 1,251      LINE 1-1 (1)
       COMMAND INPUT ===>                                      SCROLL ===> 1
       PREFIX=DSMON*  DEST=(ALL)  OWNER=*  SYSNAME=
       NP   JOBNAME  JobID     Owner     Prty C Forms    Dest              Tot-Rec
       s_   DSMON    JOB04088 ORIPOME      7 H STD        LOCAL               1,251
```

Figure 5.1   Selecting job output to display

This places you in a browse session where you can see the entire output of your job, including your interpreted JCL, system messages, and the output generated by your job.

Let's take a look at some of the default reports DSMON produces. For the complete list of
DSMON reports, see the *z/OS V1R6.0 Security Server RACF Auditor's Guide*, Topic 5.2.3,
"Functions DSMON Uses."

5.2.2 The System Report

The first report created by this execution of DSMON is the System Report, shown in Figure 5.2.
Scroll down the job output with F8 until you get to it. This report provides general system information, such as the version of the operating system, the system residence volume for the operating system, the Systems Management Facility (SMF) ID for the system, and the CPU serial
number and model. This information is roughly equivalent to the version information that typically appears at the top of the dmesg command output in UNIX.

```
       SDSF OUTPUT DISPLAY DSMON     JOB03976  DSID    101 LINE 19      COLUMNS 02- 81
       COMMAND INPUT ===> _                                            SCROLL ===> 1
       ICH66003I ICHDSM00 ENDED ON 05/17/07 AT 13:53:10 - RETURN CODE = 0
       RACF DATA SECURITY MONITOR
                                                        S Y S T E M     R E P O R T
       --------------------------------------------------------------------------------
       CPU-ID                          038717
       CPU MODEL                       2064
       OPERATING SYSTEM/LEVEL          z/OS 1.6.1
       SYSTEM RESIDENCE VOLUME         G1601B
       SMF-ID                          IP01
       RACF (FMID HRF7709) IS ACTIVE
       RACF DATA SECURITY MONITOR
```

Figure 5.2   The System Report

Think of the System Report as the "title page" or "cover" of your report. You should ask
these questions when looking at this report:

- Does it describe the correct system?
- Is the operating system at the expected level?

- Is the operating system level supported?
- Was the expected SYSRES volume used when the system was initialized? SYSRES is the DASD volume that contains the system software.

5.2.3 The Program Properties Table Report

The next report is the Program Properties Table (PPT) report, shown in Figure 5.3.

```
    SDSF OUTPUT DISPLAY DSMON      JOB03976  DSID    102 LINE 11      COLUMNS 02- 81
    COMMAND INPUT ===>  _                                            SCROLL ===> 1
                              P R O G R A M    P R O P E R T I E S     T A B L
    PROGRAM         BYPASS PASSWORD            SYSTEM
    NAME            PROTECTION                 KEY
    --------------------------------------------------------------------------------
    IEDQTCAM             NO                    YES
    ISTINM01             YES                   YES
    IKTCAS00             NO                    YES
    AHLGTF               NO                    YES
    HHLGTF               NO                    YES
    IHLGTF               NO                    YES
```

Figure 5.3   The Program Properties Table (PPT)

Entries in the PPT give programs special privileges. Note, however, that those privileges are granted to programs only if their binary is in an APF-authorized data set, a data set that is authorized for system privileges. This prevents unauthorized users from setting up their own authorized programs. For more information about APF authorized data sets, see Section 5.2.7, "The Selected Data Sets Report."

DSMON reports two of the privileges that are specified in the PPT:

- Bypass RACF access controls for data sets. Programs that can do this have a YES in the BYPASS PASSWORD PROTECTION column. The capability to bypass RACF access controls has nothing to do with passwords; the term refers back to a time when data sets were protected by passwords associated with the data set. This is roughly equivalent to running under the root user in UNIX or Linux because root can read and modify any file, regardless of permissions. By the way, this privilege is implemented not by RACF itself, but by the services that normally call RACF. RACF is bypassed completely.

- Execute in a system key. Each program that executes on z/OS has an associated storage access key. Keys 8–15 are used for programs that do not require system storage access permissions. A program that has NO in the SYSTEM KEY field is running with a user execution key. A YES in this field means that the program runs initially with a system storage protection key of 0–7 and can modify memory that the operating system itself uses. This is roughly equivalent to running as a kernel module, which is allowed to change everything on a UNIX or Linux system.

When looking at this report, ask yourself, "Are these the programs that I expect to find?" The *z/OS MVS Initialization and Tuning Reference* has a list of the IBM defaults for the PPT.

5.2.4 The RACF Authorized Caller Table (ICHAUTAB) Report

Most of the time, modules that call RACF run with system privileges of some kind. It is possible to configure RACF so that a module without any other system privileges can issue some RACF requests (RACROUTE REQUEST=LIST, which reads RACF profiles, and RACROUTE REQUEST=VERIFY, which verifies that access is allowed). The list of these modules appears in the RACF Authorized Caller Table, shown in Figure 5.4.

```
     SDSF OUTPUT DISPLAY DSMON     JOB03976  DSID    102 LINE 135     COLUMNS 02- 81
     COMMAND INPUT ===>                                               SCROLL ===> 1
                             R A C F     A U T H O R I Z E D    C A L L E R
     MODULE                RACINIT        RACLIST
     NAME                  AUTHORIZED     AUTHORIZED
     ------------------------------------------------------------------------------
     NO ENTRIES IN RACF AUTHORIZED CALLER TABLE
     RACF DATA SECURITY MONITOR
```

Figure 5.4   The RACF Authorized Called Table (ICHAUTHAB) report

This is the simplest report to review because IBM recommends that the Authorized Caller Table have no entries.

5.2.5 The RACF Exits Report

The next report DSMON produces is the RACF Exits report, which shows the RACF exits that have been defined to the system, shown in Figure 5.5. Those are hooks used to alter or augment RACF processing. They are used to add installation-specific modules to RACF, and it is important to verify that none of these modules introduces vulnerabilities.

```
     SDSF OUTPUT DISPLAY DSMON     JOB03976  DSID    102 LINE 141     COLUMNS 02- 81
     COMMAND INPUT ===> _                                             SCROLL ===> 1
                                                             R A C F     E X I T S     R E P
     EXIT MODULE           MODULE
     NAME                  LENGTH
     ------------------------------------------------------------------------------
     ICHPWX01                 16
```

Figure 5.5   The RACF Exits report

In a perfect world, there would be no need for exits. However, sometimes an installation decides to write an exit to augment how a product works. If your installation has chosen to do so, this report will list your exit. Ask yourself these questions:

- Are the exits that I expect identified? Your installation should be capable of documenting the purpose, ownership, and status of each exit.

- Do they have the expected length? An incorrect length might indicate that an unexpected change has been made to the exit.

- Are there any error messages? If an exit has been defined to RACF and it cannot be located, DSMON returns an error. The absence of an exit could cause RACF to not return the access control answer that you expect. Error messages should be reported to the systems programming staff and should be investigated.

Warning

RACF exits can be dangerous. This report provides a measure of security, but if you use any RACF exits, you should verify that you have the source code, that the exit is secure, and that the module hasn't been tampered with. To do this, you must examine the link pack area (LPA). This topic is beyond the scope of this book; for more information, see the *z/OS MVS Initialization and Tuning Reference* manual.

5.2.6 The Selected User Attribute Report

The next report is the Selected User Attribute report (shown in Figure 5.6), which is a report of all the users who have extraordinary RACF authorities. These user IDs are often the RACF administrators.

```
                              S E L E C T E D    U S E R    A T T R I B U T
        USERID            ----------------- ATTRIBUTE TYPE ----------------    -------
                          SPECIAL        OPERATIONS      AUDITOR        REVOKE    NODE.US

        -------------------------------------------------------------------------------
        BCV               SYSTEM         SYSTEM          SYSTEM
        BL                SYSTEM         SYSTEM
        BUSHICK           SYSTEM         SYSTEM
        CLINARD           SYSTEM         SYSTEM
```

Figure 5.6   The RACF Administrators report

Chapter 6, "Limited-Authority RACF Administrators," explains the different administrator attributes and their meanings. For now, it is enough that you see the list of RACF administrators and their permission levels. This is followed by a summary of the permission levels and the number of users who have them, as shown in Figure 5.7.

```
                          S E L E C T E D    U S E R    A T T R I B U T E
        -------------------------------------------------------------------------------
        TOTAL DEFINED USERS:              57
        TOTAL SELECTED ATTRIBUTE USERS:
        ATTRIBUTE BASIS       SPECIAL            OPERATIONS          AUDITOR
        ----------------    ----------------   ----------------    ----------------
        SYSTEM                    12                 14                    3
        GROUP                      0                  0                    0
```

Figure 5.7   The RACF Administrators Summary report

This report deserves a careful review. Focus on these items:

- Is the user ID IBMUSER revoked? As a predefined user ID, IBMUSER is a well-known ID that should not be used for any work after the system has been defined. IBM recommends revoking IBMUSER after you have defined other user IDs on your system. Note that the RACF_IBMUSER_REVOKED check in the IBM Health Checker for z/OS infrastructure also reports on the status of IBMUSER. Section 5.5, "The RACF Health Checks," explains the IBM Health Checker.

- Do you have any user IDs that have too much authority? In the spirit of the principles of separation of duties and least privilege, you should question any user ID that has multiple attributes that give it extraordinary authority, such as the SPECIAL, OPERATIONS, or AUDITOR attributes. You should also consider who is allowed to use these user IDs. From a separation of duties perspective, having one user who has a user ID that has SPECIAL, OPERATIONS, and AUDITOR is just as dangerous as having a user who has access to three user IDs, one that has SPECIAL, one that has OPERATIONS, and one that has AUDITOR.

- Do you have an excessive number of user IDs with any of these extraordinary authorities? There's no hard-and-fast rule for the correct number of user IDs that have the extraordinary authorities. You should be able to justify and show management approval for each user ID with an extraordinary authority.

5.2.7   The Selected Data Sets Report

The Selected Data Sets report shows many of the key system data sets for your z/OS environment, including these:

- APF-authorized data sets, which contain programs that might execute with the capability to perform restricted privileged functions. These data sets allow unauthorized users to call system services, similar to SETUID programs in UNIX and Linux.

- Link list data sets, which comprise the default program search order. These data sets are somewhat analogous to /bin and /usr/bin under UNIX and Linux.

- Catalogs, which are data sets where the data sets are "cataloged" so that they can be found more easily (such as by their name). They have some similarities to a directory, except that the data sets can be on different volumes or device types, or might not exist at all.

- Data sets that make up the RACF database.

Figure 5.8 shows this report.

```
                                          S E L E C T E D     D A T A    S E T S
                                                VOLUME      SELECTION
           DATA SET NAME                        SERIAL      CRITERION
           --------------------------------------------------------------------
           ASF.V2R1M0.SASFPLIB                  PP011P      APF
           ASF.V2R1M0.SASFPLNK                  PP011P      LNKLST
           ASM.SASMMOD1                         G1601D      LNKLST
           BBO.V4R0M1.SBBOLD2                   PP064P      APF
           BBO.V4R0M1.SBBOLOAD                  PP064P      APF
           BBO.V4R0M1.SBBOLPA                   PP064P      APF
           CATALOG.COMN01                       COMN01      USER CATALOG
           CATALOG.DPQTOA                       DPQTOA      USER CATALOG
           CATALOG.DPQTOB                       DPQTOB      USER CATALOG
           CATALOG.DPTFAT                       DPTFAT      USER CATALOG
           CATALOG.DPTITM                       DPTITM      USER CATALOG
           CATALOG.DPTI91                       DPTI91      USER CATALOG
           CATALOG.DPTLFN                       DPTLFN      USER CATALOG
           CATALOG.DPTNV1                       DPTNV1      USER CATALOG
```

Figure 5.8   The Selected Data Sets report

Table 5.2 explains the data fields in the data set report.

Table 5.2   Fields in the Data Set Report

Field Name	Meaning
Data Set Name	The full name of the data set.
Volume Serial	The serial number of the volume that contains the data set.
Selection Criterion	The reason this data set is part of the report.
RACF Indicated	Is there a discrete profile for this data set? N.F. indicates that the data set could not be found on the volume. N.M. means that the volume is not mounted.
RACF Protected	Is the data set protected by any profile? If the data set is RACF protected but not RACF indicated, it means that access to it is specified by a generic profile.
UACC	Default permission level.

This report contains a lot of information. Be sure to review these key items:

- Are the data sets listed the data sets you expected to see? Additional data sets might represent an inadvertent extension of the operating system.

- Why are data sets shown as not found (N.F.) or not mounted (N.M.)? What controls are in place to ensure that unauthorized users will not allocate data sets with those names?

- Is the UACC value consistent with the data contained within the data set? For example, it makes sense to allow everybody to read an APF data set, which contains programs. It does not make sense to allow everybody to read a data set with payroll information.

- Is the access list for the data set consistent with the installation security policy? Note that "RACF protected" means only that a RACF profile protects the resource. That profile could allow access to users who should not have access to the resource.

Tip

Check for additional information on APF data sets, link list data sets, PARMLIB data sets, and
RACF database data sets. See Section 5.6, "The RACF Health Checks."

5.3 The Set RACF Options (`SETROPTS`) Command

As part of a z/OS audit, review the RACF options in effect on your system. To do that, use this
TSO command:

```
SETROPTS LIST
```

This command can create hundreds of lines of output. To capture the output, run the TSO
command interpreter (`IKJEFT01`) in a batch job and give it the command as input, as shown in
Listing 5.2. You can use the short version of the command, `SETR`.

Listing 5.2   JCL Job to List RACF Options

```
//SETROPTS   JOB   CLASS=A,NOTIFY=&SYSUID,MSGCLASS=H
//SETROPTS   EXEC  PGM=IKJEFT01,DYNAMNBR=100
//SYSTSPRT   DD    SYSOUT=*
//SYSPRINT   DD    SYSOUT=*
//SYSTSIN    DD    *
 SETR LIST
/*
```

The list of RACF options shows many different aspects of the RACF environment. This
section explains the most important ones. For a complete description, see *z/OS Security Server
RACF Command Language Reference,* Topic 5.30, "`SETROPTS` (Set RACF Options)"; and *z/OS
Security Server RACF Security Administrator's Guide*, Chapter 5, "Specifying RACF Options."

The attributes line, shown in Figure 5.9, contains a number of log settings. In most cases,
those settings should be on.

- **SAUDIT**—Does RACF log the actions of RACF administrators, users with the
  `system-SPECIAL` attribute?
- **CMDVIOL**—Does RACF log RACF command violations, unauthorized attempts to
  change RACF profiles?
- **OPERAUDIT**—Does RACF log the actions of RACF operators, users with the
  `system-OPERATOR` attribute?
- **INITSTATS**—Does RACF record the last logon date and time of each user?

```
READY
  SETR LIST
ATTRIBUTES = INITSTATS WHEN(PROGRAM -- BASIC) SAUDIT CMDVIOL NOOPERAUDIT
```

Figure 5.9 Attributes in the RACF options

The WHEN(PROGRAM) attribute indicates that RACF program control is activated. For more information about this function, see *z/OS Security Server RACF Security Administrator's Guide,* Chapter 9, "Protecting Programs."

SETROPTS lists each of the RACF general resource classes that are active, as shown in Figure 5.10. RACF access control and logging are active for only those resource classes. Check your security policy to ensure that no classes are missing.

```
ACTIVE CLASSES = DATASET USER GROUP ACCTNUM CBIND CIMS DIMS FACILITY FIELD
                 GXFACILI LOGSTRM PTKTDATA PTKTVAL RODMMGR SCDMBR SECDATA
                 SECLABEL SECLMBR SERVER STARTED TSOAUTH TSOPROC UNIXPRIV
                 XFACILIT
```

Figure 5.10 Active RACF classes

RACF enables installations to specify the protection of data sets that are not protected by a profile, using the PROTECTALL option (shown in Figure 5.11). Three possible settings exist for PROTECTALL.

- **NOPROTECTALL**—Open access by default. Access is always allowed unless there is a protection profile.
- **PROTECTALL(WARN)**—If there is no protection profile, access is allowed, but with a warning message (ICH408I) to the user and the security administrator.
- **PROTECTALL(FAIL)**—Closed access by default. Access is always denied unless a protection profile allows it. This is the proper setting for a production system.

```
PROTECT-ALL OPTION IS NOT IN EFFECT
```

Figure 5.11 The PROTECTALL option

Figure 5.12 shows the password options. The settings are self-explanatory, but for more details, you can look at the *z/OS Security Server RACF Security Administrator's Guide,* Topics 5.2.1–5.2.3.

```
PASSWORD PROCESSING OPTIONS:
   PASSWORD CHANGE INTERVAL IS  30 DAYS.
   NO PASSWORD HISTORY BEING MAINTAINED.
   USERIDS NOT BEING AUTOMATICALLY REVOKED.
   NO PASSWORD EXPIRATION WARNING MESSAGES WILL BE ISSUED.
   NO INSTALLATION PASSWORD SYNTAX RULES ARE PRESENT.
```

Figure 5.12 Password options

Unused user IDs are a security risk. A hacker could break into them and nobody would notice. On production systems, it is a good idea to automatically revoke those accounts. Figure 5.12 was taken from a test system on which security is not an issue.

5.4 The RACF Database Unload Utility (IRRDBU00)

In Chapter 4, you learned about the RACF SMF Unload Utility, IRRADU00. This utility translates security-related SMF records (SMF types 30, 80, 81, and 83) into an ordered data set of records, similar to a file under UNIX or Windows. This data set is suitable for processing using virtually any report-generation package, browsing using an editor, or loading into a relation database manager of your choice.

The RACF Database Unload Utility, IRRDBU00, does the same for the RACF database. IRRDBU00 can be run using the live primary RACF database, the live backup RACF database, or an offline copy of the RACF database. IBM recommends running the utility against an offline copy of the RACF database, for performance reasons. Many installations run IRRDBU00 as a part of their daily backup of the RACF database.

To identify the location of the RACF database and any live backups, use the TSO command RVARY LIST, as shown in Figure 5.13.

```
READY
RVARY LIST
ICH15013I RACF DATABASE STATUS:
ACTIVE    USE    NUMBER    VOLUME       DATASET
------    ---    ------    ------       -------
 YES      PRIM      1      RO1221       SYS1.NMP122.RACF
ICH15020I RVARY COMMAND HAS FINISHED PROCESSING.
READY
```

Figure 5.13   RACF databases

Listing 5.3 shows the JCL to run IRRDBU00. Use the name of your live backup RACF database, to provide the latest information, in the INDD1 data definition. Enter this JCL into RACFBK.CNTL(UNLRACF) and submit it.

> **Warning**
>
> We unload from a live database because we assume that you are running the exercises on a test system where performance is not an issue. If you are using a production machine, ask where the offline backup is located.

Listing 5.3   JCL Job to Unload the Live RACF Database

```
//UNLRACF   JOB   CLASS=A,NOTIFY=&SYSUID,MSGCLASS=H
//UNLRACF   EXEC  PGM=IRRDBU00,PARM=NOLOCK
//INDD1     DD    DISP=SHR,DSN=SYS1.NMP122.RACF
//OUTDD     DD    DISP=(MOD,CATLG,DELETE),DSN=&SYSUID..RACF.UNLOAD,
//                UNIT=SYSALLDA,DCB=(RECFM=VB,LRECL=8096,BLKSIZE=0),
//                SPACE=(CYL,(10,10))
//SYSPRINT  DD    SYSOUT=*
```

The `IRRDBU00` program uses these data definitions:

- **INDD1, INDD2 … INDDn**—Your input RACF data set. If your RACF database is stored in a single data set, use `INDD1`. If it is split among multiple data sets, use `INDD2`, `INDD3`, and so on.

- **OUTDD**—The output data set for the unloaded records. `IRRDBU00` expects this data set to have a record format of `VB` (variable-length records in blocks) with a maximum record length of at least 8,096. The data definition in Listing 5.3 creates such a data set.

- **SYSPRINT**—Messages produced by `IRRDBU00`. Those are the kind of messages that a UNIX program would put in stderr.

For more information about unloading RACF databases, read the *z/OS Security Server RACF Security Administrator's Guide,* Chapter 11, "Working with the RACF Database." To see how to analyze the unloaded records using ICETOOL, see the examples in `SYS1.` `SAMPLIB(IRRICE)`.

5.4.1   Removing IDs with `IRRRID00`

One important use for unloaded RACF databases is to identify and delete references to nonexistent users and groups. To do this, use the RACF remove ID utility, `IRRRID00`. This utility has two modes:

1. **Residual IDs**—These are IDs that are used improperly, such as deleted IDs that still appear in ACLs or group IDs that appear where a user ID is required. Deleted IDs that appear in ACLs are a serious risk because if another ID is created with the same name, it will have unintended permissions.

2. **Specified IDs**—IDs specified in `SYSIN`.

Listing 5.4 has two job steps to show the use of IRRRID00 in both modes.

Listing 5.4   JCL Job to Identify References to Users

```
//DELIDS    JOB  CLASS=A,NOTIFY=&SYSUID,MSGCLASS=H
//RESIDIDS EXEC PGM=IRRRID00
//SYSPRINT DD   SYSOUT=*
//SYSOUT    DD   SYSOUT=*
//SORTOUT   DD   UNIT=SYSALLDA,SPACE=(CYL,(5,5))
//SYSUT1    DD   UNIT=SYSALLDA,SPACE=(CYL,(3,3))
//INDD      DD   DISP=OLD,DSN=&SYSUID..RACF.UNLOAD
//OUTDD     DD   DISP=(MOD,CATLG,DELETE),DSN=&SYSUID..RESIDS.CLIST,
//               UNIT=SYSALLDA,DCB=(RECFM=VB,LRECL=1024,BLKSIZE=0),
//               SPACE=(CYL,(5,5))
//SYSIN     DD   DUMMY
//SPECIDS  EXEC PGM=IRRRID00
//SYSPRINT DD   SYSOUT=*
//SYSOUT    DD   SYSOUT=*
//SORTOUT   DD   UNIT=SYSALLDA,SPACE=(CYL,(5,5))
//SYSUT1    DD   UNIT=SYSALLDA,SPACE=(CYL,(3,3))
//INDD      DD   DISP=OLD,DSN=&SYSUID..RACF.UNLOAD
//OUTDD     DD   DISP=(MOD,CATLG,DELETE),DSN=&SYSUID..SPECIDS.CLIST,
//               UNIT=SYSALLDA,DCB=(RECFM=VB,LRECL=1024,BLKSIZE=0),
//               SPACE=(CYL,(5,5))
//SYSIN     DD   *
 MYUSER
/*
```

This job has two job steps, RESIDIDS and SPECIDS. Both jobs use two temporary data sets, SORTOUT and SYSUT1. Because these are temporary data sets, we let JES assign names for them. If you look at the job output in Figure 5.14, you will see the names used and the fact that they were deleted.

```
 SDSF OUTPUT DISPLAY DELIDS    JOB04027   DSID    4 LINE 40      COLUMNS 01- 80
 COMMAND INPUT ===> _                                           SCROLL ===> 1
 IEF285I    ORIPOME.DELIDS.JOB04027.D0000102.?            SYSOUT
 IEF285I    ORIPOME.DELIDS.JOB04027.D0000103.?            SYSOUT
 IGD105I SYS07200.T111713.RA000.DELIDS.R0100069           DELETED,    DDNAME=SORTOUT
 IGD105I SYS07200.T111713.RA000.DELIDS.R0100070           DELETED,    DDNAME=SYSUT1
 IGD104I ORIPOME.RACF.UNLOAD                              RETAINED,   DDNAME=INDD
 IGD104I ORIPOME.RESIDS.CLIST                             RETAINED,   DDNAME=OUTDD
```

Figure 5.14   Temporary data sets in the job output

The output of `IRRRID00` is a command list, written to `OUTDD`. After you review it and modify it as needed, you can execute it to remove the user IDs and references to them. In the job in Listing 5.4, that output is written to data sets `RESIDS.CLIST` (for residual IDs) and `SPECIDS.CLIST` (for specified IDs).

On a well-configured system, `RESIDS.CLIST` should not have anything interesting. `SPECIDS.CLIST`, on the other hand, would have the commands to delete MYUSER and all the references to it, as shown in Figure 5.15.

Notice the `EXIT` command before the line that actually deletes the user. To avoid mistakes through carelessness, you must delete that line to actually remove the user.

```
PERMIT    'TEXTS.*.*' GENERIC  ID(MYUSER  ) DELETE
PERMIT    USER.TSO.*  CLASS(FIELD   ) ID(MYUSER  ) DELETE
PERMIT    FINCONF  CLASS(SECLABEL ) ID(MYUSER  ) DELETE

/*******************************************************************/
/* The following commands delete profiles.  You must review       */
/* these commands, editing them if necessary, and then remove     */
/* the EXIT statement to allow the execution of the commands.     */
/*******************************************************************/

EXIT

DELUSER  MYUSER
```

Figure 5.15   Command list generated by `IRRRID00`

If a user owns a resource, deleting this user requires an administrator to decide who will be the new owner. `IRRRID00` still produces the commands, but with `?<deleted user ID>` in the fields that need to be replaced. For example, Figure 5.16 shows part of the output of `IRRRID00` on the user used as the RACF administrator in this book. To remove this user, you must first come up with alternative owners to everything it owns and insert those owners to the commands.

```
ALTGROUP TEXTS      OWNER(?ORIPOME )
CONNECT  MYUSER     GROUP(OMVS     ) OWNER(?ORIPOME )
CONNECT  MYUSER     GROUP(TEXTS    ) OWNER(?ORIPOME )
ALTUSER  MYUSER     OWNER(?ORIPOME )
ALTDSD   'LIBRARY.B*.*' GENERIC  OWNER(?ORIPOME )
PERMIT   USER.TSO.*  CLASS(FIELD   ) ID(ORIPOME ) DELETE
RALTER   FIELD      USER.TSO.* OWNER(?ORIPOME )
```

Figure 5.16   `IRRRID00` identifies resources that will need a new owner

To execute the command, run the TSO interpreter, as you saw earlier in Listing 5.2. Change the `SYSIN` definition to the data set `IRRRID00` creates.

5.5 The RACF Health Checks

IBM Health Checker for z/OS is a new feature in z/OS V1R7. This feature allows z/OS components such as RACF to write checks that are then managed by the Health Checker infrastructure. Several of the RACF checks are relevant to audits.

Checks are defined with a default severity and execution interval. Your installation can change the severity and interval, or can disable a check entirely. Details on installing and tailoring the IBM Health Checker for z/OS are in the *IBM Health Checker for z/OS Users Guide.*

5.5.1 `RACF_SENSITIVE_RESOURCES`

The first of these checks is the `RACF_SENSITIVE_RESOURCES` check, which reports on various key z/OS resources.

`RACF_SENSITIVE_RESOURCES` reports on the following sensitive data sets:

- **APF list**—Data sets with programs that can be executed as authorized, roughly equivalent to the list of programs with set UID in UNIX

- **PARMLIB concatenation**—Data sets with operating system parameters, roughly equivalent to the content of the `/etc` directory

- **LINKLIST concatenation**—Data sets with programs, roughly equivalent to the default path

- **RACF database**—Data sets that contain the RACF database

For all these data sets, the check examines the RACF protection attributes of the data set. It flags exceptions if data sets have

- **Inappropriate UACC**—Universal access that compromises the security of z/OS. For example, most users should not be allowed READ access on the RACF database. They should not be allowed UPDATE access for the other data sets that `RACF_SENSITIVE_ RESOURCES` checks.

- **Inappropriate ID(*) ACL entry**—Such an ACL entry applies to all RACF-authenticated users. Any access level that is inappropriate in UACC is inappropriate for `ID(*)`.

- **Warning mode profile**—RACF protection profiles can either forbid access (fail mode) or allow it and issue a warning to the user and the system log (warning mode). Warning mode prevents downtime in the case of RACF configuration errors, but it is not appropriate for the sensitive data sets.

`RACF_SENSITIVE_RESOURCES` also checks access to sensitive general resource, such as `SUPERUSER.FILESYS.SUPERUSER`, `SUPERUSER.FILESYS.CHANGEPERMS`, and `SUPERUSER. FILESYS.CHOWN` in the `UNIXPRIV` class. The full list of sensitive resources is available in the check report itself.

To see the result of the health check, go to SDSF and select CK. Use s to select the appropriate check from the list, as shown in Figure 5.17. If the option CK is not available on the SDSF menu, it means your system programmer did not configure health checks; ask him or her to do so.

```
    SDSF HEALTH CHECKER DISPLAY  RACFR17              LINE 22-42 (62)
    COMMAND INPUT ===>                                    SCROLL ===> PAGE
 NP   NAME                        CheckOwner       State              Status
      PDSE_SMSPDSE1               IBMPDSE          ACTIVE(ENABLED)    EXCEPT
      RACF_FACILITY_ACTIVE        IBMRACF          ACTIVE(ENABLED)    EXCEPT
      RACF_GRS_RNL                IBMRACF          ACTIVE(DISABLED)   ENV N/
      RACF_IBMUSER_REVOKED        IBMRACF          ACTIVE(ENABLED)    EXCEPT
      RACF_OPERCMDS_ACTIVE        IBMRACF          ACTIVE(ENABLED)    EXCEPT
  s   RACF_SENSITIVE_RESOURCES    IBMRACF          ACTIVE(ENABLED)    EXCEPT
      RACF_TAPEVOL_ACTIVE         IBMRACF          ACTIVE(ENABLED)    EXCEPT
      RACF_TEMPDSN_ACTIVE         IBMRACF          ACTIVE(ENABLED)    EXCEPT
      RACF_TSOAUTH_ACTIVE         IBMRACF          ACTIVE(ENABLED)    SUCCES
      RACF_UNIXPRIV_ACTIVE        IBMRACF          ACTIVE(ENABLED)    EXCEPT
```

Figure 5.17 Health checks list

Selecting a check from the CK panel shows the health check's results. Figure 5.18 shows part of the results for the APF data sets. Notice that no characters exist in the status column, the first column on the left. This means that no exceptions were found.

```
    SDSF OUTPUT DISPLAY RACF_SENSITIVE_RESOURCES    LINE 0      COLUMNS 02- 81
    COMMAND INPUT ===> _                                        SCROLL ===> PAGE
    ********************************* TOP OF DATA *********************************
    CHECK(IBMRACF,RACF_SENSITIVE_RESOURCES)
    START TIME: 07/24/2007 15:20:45.781105
    CHECK DATE: 20040703  CHECK SEVERITY: HIGH

                      APF Dataset Report

 S Data Set Name                      Vol    UACC Warn ID* User
 - ------------------------------     ------ ---- ---- ---- ----
   AAAAAAAA.APFLIB                    TEMP01 None No   ****
   ASM.SASMMOD1                       ZDR17  None No   ****
   CBC.SCLBDLL                        ZDR17
   CBC.SCLBDLL2                       ZDR17
   CEE.SCEERUN                        ZDR17
```

Figure 5.18 Health check results

You can specify a user ID as a parameter to the RACF_SENSITIVE_RESOURCES check. That user ID has its access tested to these data sets, and an exception is raised if the user ID has access that would exceed that of a normal user.

Health checks are executed as operator commands. However, they are too long to enter on the SDSF command line. Instead, type / on the SDSF command line and press Enter. SDSF opens a large prompt for an operator command. In that prompt, type the following command, as shown in Figure 5.19:

```
F HC,UPDATE,CHECK=(IBMRACF,RACF_SENSITIVE _RESOURCES),PARM=<user>
```

```
   HQX7720 ---------------- SDSF PRIMARY OPTION MENU  ------------------------
   COMMAND INPUT ===>                                     SCROLL ===> PAGE
   .----------------------------------------------------------------.
 DA |                                                                |
 I  |                   System Command Extension                     |
 O  |                                                                |
 H  |   Type or complete typing a system command, press Enter.       |
 ST |                                                                |
    |        ===> F HC,UPDATE,CHECK=(IBMRACF,RACF_SENSITIVE_         |
 LOG|        ===> RESOURCES),PARM=MARKN_                             |
 SR |        ===>                                                    |
 MAS|                                                                |
 JC '----------------------------------------------------------------'
 SE  Scheduling environments          CK    Health checker
 RES WLM resources
 ENC Enclaves                         ULOG  User session log
 PS  Processes

 END Exit SDSF
```

Figure 5.19   Running a health check from SDSF with a parameter

Figure 5.20 shows the results of the health check. Note that the two top data sets have E in the status column. This means that MARKN has too much access for a regular user.

```
   SDSF OUTPUT DISPLAY RACF_SENSITIVE_RESOURCES      LINE 0       COLUMNS 02- 81
   COMMAND INPUT ===>                                          SCROLL ===> PAGE
   ******************************** TOP OF DATA ********************************
   CHECK(IBMRACF,RACF_SENSITIVE_RESOURCES)
   START TIME: 07/24/2007 15:25:42.748963
   CHECK DATE: 20040703  CHECK SEVERITY: HIGH
   CHECK PARM: MARKN
                             .

                          APF Dataset Report

   S Data Set Name                     Vol    UACC Warn ID* User
   - -------------------------------- ------ ---- ---- ---- ----
   E AAAAAAAA.APFLIB                   TEMP01 None No   **** >Read
   E ASM.SASMMOD1                      ZDR17  None No   **** >Read
     CBC.SCLBDLL                       ZDR17
     CBC.SCLBDLL2                      ZDR17
```

Figure 5.20   Health check with an administrator as a parameter

Resources that are flagged either have improper access, have no access control, or are data sets located on a different volume than the expected one. If a resource is not protected by a profile, the UACC, Warn, and ID* columns will be empty (as is the case with CBC.SCLBDLL in Figure 5.20). If that causes exceptions, either create the appropriate profiles or change the RACF properties to protect all the resources using PROTECTALL(FAIL), as explained in Chapter 3, "Protecting Data Sets and Other Resources." Because a change of this magnitude can have wide-ranging results, do not move to PROTECTALL(FAIL) without careful planning.

5.5.2 RACF_IBMUSER_REVOKED

When RACF is first installed, the only user ID that is defined is IBMUSER. During the RACF installation process, this user is used to define other user IDs. After this is done, IBMUSER should be revoked. People who try to break into mainframes often try to use this account because it has permissions to administer RACF.

By convention, when IBM Health Checker for z/OS raises an exception, the report includes everything that appears in the product's *Messages and Codes* manual, including the solution. Figure 5.21 shows the health check report when IBMUSER is active.

```
CHECK(IBMRACF,RACF_IBMUSER_REVOKED)
START TIME: 07/23/2007 18:05:08.344546
CHECK DATE: 20051111  CHECK SEVERITY: MEDIUM

* Medium Severity Exception *

IRRH225E The user ID IBMUSER is not revoked.

  Explanation:  The user ID IBMUSER has not been revoked. IBM recommends
    revoking IBMUSER.

  System Action:  The check continues processing. There is no effect on
    the system.

  Operator Response:  Report this problem to the system security
    administrator and the system auditor.

  System Programmer Response:  Revoke IBMUSER.
```

Figure 5.21   Health check report for RACF_IBMUSER_REVOKED with the solution

5.5.3 RACF Classes Active Health Checks

For RACF to protect z/OS properly, several general resource classes should be active:

- **FACILITY**—Protects various z/OS subsystems
- **OPERCMDS**—Restricts access to specific commands for specific users to specified consoles
- **TAPEVOL**—Restricts access to data sets on tape
- **TEMPDSN**—Restricts access to temporary data sets created by jobs that are aborted (for example, because of hardware failures)
- **TSOAUTH**—Restricts TSO user authorities
- **UNIXPRIV**—Grants specific OMVS privileges instead of the UNIX superuser

For each of these classes there is a health check that verifies it is active. Figure 5.22 shows the health check for an active class. Note that an active class is a necessary condition for security, but not a sufficient one. After the class is activated, the RACF administrator needs to create the appropriate resource profiles to actually restrict access to authorized users.

```
******************************* TOP OF DATA *************************************
CHECK(IBMRACF,RACF_TSOAUTH_ACTIVE)
START TIME: 07/23/2007 18:05:08.344075
CHECK DATE: 20051111   CHECK SEVERITY: MEDIUM
CHECK PARM: TSOAUTH


IRRH228I The class TSOAUTH is active.

END TIME: 07/23/2007 18:05:08.347833   STATUS: SUCCESSFUL
****************************** BOTTOM OF DATA ***********************************
```

Figure 5.22   Health check report for an active class

Tip

Before activating a class, be sure to review the implications of having the class active. For example, the TEMPDSN class should not be activated while the z/OS is processing a job that might have a temporary data set allocated.

5.6 zSecure Auditing

zSecure includes a number of audit reports. Type **AU.S** and then select the type of entity you want to audit, as shown in Figure 5.23.

```
                        zSecure Suite - Audit - Status
    Command ===> _____

    Enter / to select report categories
    _  MVS tables         MVS oriented tables (reads first part of CKFREEZE)
    _  MVS extended       MVS oriented tables (reads whole CKFREEZE)
    _  RACF control       RACF oriented tables
    /  RACF user          User oriented RACF tables and reports
    _  RACF resource      Resource oriented RACF tables and reports
```

Figure 5.23   Selecting entity type to audit in zSecure

Then you select from a list of preconfigured audit reports. Figure 5.24 shows part of the list of reports about users.

```
zSecure Suite Display Selection                              Line 1 of 24
Command ===> _____  Scroll===> 0001

   Name      Summary Records Title
_  TRUSTUSR     1     3541 Trusted userids (may bypass security)
_  AUTHSYS      1      123 Users with system-wide special, operations, auditor,
_  AUTHUID0     1       43 Users with uid 0
/  AUTHGRP      1       43 Users with group level special, operations, auditor
_  SHRDUIDS     1      154 OMVS UIDs shared between RACF users
_  OMVSNUID     1       10 RACF users with OMVS segment but no UID
_  SHRDGIDS     1       35 OMVS GIDs shared between RACF groups
_  OMVSNGID     1        3 RACF groups with OMVS segment but no GID
_  PROTECT      1     2524 Protected users
```

Figure 5.24   Selecting a user audit report in zSecure

Then you get a report, such as the group authorities report shown in Figure 5.25.

```
Users with group level special, operations, auditor         Line 1 of 43
Command ===> _____  Scroll===> 0001
                                             6 Sep 2007 15:01
   Complex  Timestamp      Group authorized Grpspecial Grpoper Grpauditor
   ED02       6Sep2007 15:01           43        39       10       12
   Userid    Name            Owner    RIRP soa LastUse LastPwd LastPhr Inst
s_ CRMAINT   TIVOLI GROUP ADMIN CRMA   ____ YY  31Jan07 31Jan07
_  CRMAROB   VAN, ROB          CRMA    ____ Y   18Jun07 5Jun07           015-
_  CRMBERT   BERT LIND         RCCSLIN ____ Y Y 22May07 22May07          ____
_  CRMBER2   BERT LIND         CRMB    ____ YYY 19Jun07 22May07          ____
_  CRMBER3   BERT LIND         CRMB    ____ Y   28May01 10Feb00          XACT
```

Figure 5.25   zSecure group-level authorities report

If you need more information about a specific line in a zSecure audit report, use the S line command. For example, Figure 5.26 shows the groups that CRMAINT has authorities for and what those authorities are.

```
Users with group level special, operations, auditor         Line 1 of 5
Command ===> _____  Scroll===> 0001
                                             6 Sep 2007 15:01
   Complex  Timestamp      Group authorized Grpspecial Grpoper Grpauditor
   ED02       6Sep2007 15:01           43        39       10       12
   Userid    Name            Owner    RIRP soa LastUse LastPwd LastPhr Inst
   CRMAINT   TIVOLI GROUP ADMIN CRMA        YY  31Jan07 31Jan07
   User/Grp Auth    R SOA AG Uacc   Revokedt    Resumedt
_  CRMA     CREATE  _ S _ NONE    _____ _____
_  CRMB     USE     _ S _ NONE    _____ _____
_  CRMC     USE     _ S _ NONE    _____ _____
_  CRMD     USE     _ O _ NONE    _____ _____
_  CRMGRACF USE     _ S _ NONE    _____ _____
********************************* Bottom of Data *********************************
```

Figure 5.26   zSecure report details

The intent of this chapter has been to provide you with a sample of some of what an auditor reviews as a part of a z/OS audit and how you can use RACF facilities to get the auditor useful information. This chapter is not intended to be a comprehensive list of what a good auditor looks for, so don't be surprised if the auditor asks you for other information, such as operational procedures, lists of applications, and data store information.

5.7 Additional Information

For additional information on auditing RACF, check out these resources:

- *z/OS Security Server RA CF Auditor's Guide,* which explains DSMON
- *An Introduction to DSMON,* which explains DSMON with a slightly different slant, available at ftp://ftp.software.ibm.com/eserver/zseries/zos/racf/pdf/r05_dsmon_introduction.pdf
- *IBM Health Checker for z/OS Users Guide,* for complete details on the IBM Health Checker for z/OS and the checks that IBM ships with z/OS
- *z/OS MVS Initialization and Tuning Reference,* for information on the z/OS initialization parameters, IBM recommended defaults, and the link pack area (LPA)
- *z/OS Security Server RACF Macros and Interfaces,* which has a complete mapping of the output of the records produced by IRRDBU00
- *z/OS Security Server RACF Systems Programmer's Guide,* which explains DSMON
- *z/OS Security Server RACF Security Administrator's Guide,* which explains IRRDBU00 and IRRRID00
- *Mainframe Audit News,* available at www.stuhenderson.com/MANEWS01.pdf

Limited-Authority RACF Administrators

Each installation needs to have a small number of superusers with unlimited powers. Typically, a much higher number of RACF administrators would be authorized to perform limited actions, such as adding users to a specific group or managing permissions to specific data sets. In this chapter, you learn how to plan and create such limited-authority RACF administrators.

6.1 Profiles Owned by Users

The RACF profile owner is a user or group that manages access to that resource. This is different than the owner of the actual resource, which is the user or group whose name is the first component of the name of the resource.

If the profile owner is a user, he or she is authorized to do anything to the profile that controls access to that resource. To see this feature in action, log on as MYUSER. Go to the RACF main menu, then choose `1.2` to change a data set profile. Choose to change `'<your user name>.RACFBK.CNTL'`. Remember, the single quotes are necessary; otherwise, ISPF will interpret the data set name as `MYUSER.<your user name>.RACFBK.CNTL`. Choose, for example, to change the owner to MYUSER. This will fail, as shown in Figure 6.1.

```
ICH22005I NOT AUTHORIZED TO ALTER ORIPOME.RACFBK.CNTL
***
```

Figure 6.1 MYUSER can't change the profile.

Now, in a different window, log on as yourself. Choose to change RACBK.CNTL's owner to MYUSER, as shown in Figure 6.2.

```
                         RACF - CHANGE DATA SET PROFILE
   COMMAND ===>

     PROFILE: RACFBK.CNTL

   ENTER THE DESIRED CHANGES:
     OWNER                ===>  myuser      Userid or group name
     LEVEL                ===>              0-99
     FAILED ACCESSES      ===>              FAIL or WARN
```

Figure 6.2   Changing the resource owner for RACFBK.CNTL to MYUSER

Now try to change the profile as MYUSER again. Because MYUSER is already the profile owner, change the ERASE ON DELETE to YES. This should work—choose **D** to display the profile to verify that, as shown in Figure 6.3.

```
   BROWSE - RACF COMMAND OUTPUT---------------------- LINE 00000000 COL 001 080
   ******************************** Top of Data ********************************
   INFORMATION FOR DATASET ORIPOME.RACFBK.CNTL

   LEVEL   OWNER    UNIVERSAL ACCESS   WARNING   ERASE
   -----   -------- ----------------   -------   -----
   00      MYUSER           NONE          NO      YES
```

Figure 6.3   The modified profile

As the profile owner, MYUSER can now modify the access control list (ACL) and universal access level (UACC) and gain access to '<your user name>.RACFBK.CNTL'. Note that without changing those fields, MYUSER still cannot access the actual data set—the ownership is limited to the RACF profile.

6.2 Group-Owned Profiles and Group Authorities

User ownership of profiles is discouraged. If the user leaves the company, nobody will be able to change the profile until an unlimited administrator changes the profile owner. Best practices are to have a group own the profile instead.

If a group owns a profile, it does not mean that everybody in that group can do whatever they want with that profile. Instead, each user who is connected to the group has some level of permission to each profile. Four standard levels of group authority exist, which affect a user's ability to access and modify group resources:

- **Use**—Use the resources of the group. A user with this level can access the shared resources of the group. For example, a user with this level might be able to read a group data set, a data set that belongs to the group (depending on the ACL).

- **Create**—Adds the right to create new data sets that will be accessible by members of this group. Typically, you would give this permission level to someone in the group who is responsible for configuring new applications.

- **Connect**—Adds the right to add existing users to the group. This might be given to a manager or team lead who needs to add existing users to the group when the job role requires access.

- **Join**—Adds the right to create new users (who will be members of the group), the right to add new subgroups, and the right to change users' permission level on the group. This might be a human resources person who needs to be able to define new users.

In addition to these group access levels, a user can have three special types of authority for profiles owned by a group. Each provides different privileges for users who have them—but only for profiles owned by that group or its subgroups.

- **group-AUDITOR**—This authority grants privileges related to auditing. It enables users to specify what information will be audited, to read and delete auditing information, and so on. This is separate from `group-OPERATIONS` to allow for separation of duties. This prevents rogue operators from erasing the traces of their actions or even knowing whether their actions leave a trace.

- **group-SPECIAL**—This authority grants the right to assign users permissions and modify RACF profiles.

- **group-OPERATIONS**—This authority grants the right to read and modify data sets, bypassing the UACC and ACL. As usual on the mainframe, there are exceptions to this, as explained in Topic 3.4.5.3 of *z/OS V1R7.0 Security Server RACF Security Administrator's Guide*. Note that it is recommended to use ACLs for this purpose instead of the group permission.

If a profile belongs to a group, the group-level permissions of that group apply to that profile. So do the permissions of the group's ancestors in the group inheritance hierarchy. For example, in

Figure 6.4, group EARTH owns groups AMERICA and EUROPE, group AMERICA owns groups US and CANADA, and group CANADA owns groups ONTARIO and MANITOBA. Users with the `group-AUDITOR` authority on MANITOBA, CANADA, AMERICA, or EARTH can audit profiles that MANITOBA owns.

If a profile is owned by a user who is owned by a group, the group authorities for that group—and any group above it—apply to that profile. For example, if ONTARIO owns JOE, then profiles JOE owns can be managed by users with group authority in ONTARIO, CANADA, AMERICA, or EARTH.

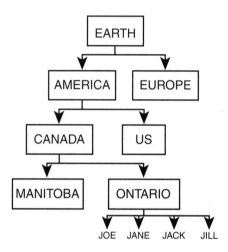

Figure 6.4   The inheritance of group privileges

Inheritance is explained in greater detail in Topic 3.4.6.1 of *z/OS V1R7.0 Security Server RACF Security Administrator's Guide.*

6.2.1 The `group-AUDITOR` Authority

The `group-AUDITOR` authority enables users to see the RACF profiles of a group and set certain auditing options. It is appropriate for auditors, managers, and other people who need to see what happens with a group's resources but who should not be able to modify them.

To see the effects of group ownership of resources and `group-AUDITOR`, use the TEXTS group you created in Chapter 3, "Protecting Data Sets and Other Resources." Choose option **3** from the main RACF menu to modify groups, enter the group's name, and choose option **4** to connect a user to it. After you type the user's name (MYUSER) and press **Enter**, you will see a screen with the group authorities. Give MYUSER `group-AUDITOR`, as shown in Figure 6.5.

```
                        RACF - ADD OR CHANGE CONNECTION TO TEXTS
        COMMAND ===>

        TO ALLOW USER ATTRIBUTES, ENTER YES
        TO DENY  USER ATTRIBUTES, ENTER NO

            GROUP ACCESS        ===>          Allow the group to access new group
                                              data sets

            ADSP                ===>          Create discrete profiles for new
                                              permanent data sets

            REVOKE              ===>          YES, mm/dd/yy (date), or blank

            RESUME              ===>          YES, mm/dd/yy (date), or blank

            SPECIAL             ===>          Grant group-SPECIAL attribute

            OPERATIONS          ===>          Grant group-OPERATIONS attribute

            AUDITOR             ===> yes      Grant group-AUDITOR attribute
```

Figure 6.5 Giving MYUSER group-AUDITOR

Next, delete the TEXTS data set profiles: 'TEXTS.*.*' and 'TEXTS.B*.*' (remember the single quotes). You can do this using these TSO commands:

```
DELDSD 'TEXTS.*.* ' GENERIC
DELDSD 'TEXTS.B*.*' GENERIC
```

> **Note**
>
> These are TSO commands. To run them from ISPF, prefix them with TSO.

Create a new 'TEXTS.*.*' generic profile that TEXTS owns and gives nobody access, as shown in Figure 6.6.

```
                            RACF - ADD DATA SET PROFILE
        COMMAND ===>

           PROFILE: 'TEXTS.*.*'

        ENTER OR CHANGE THE FOLLOWING INFORMATION:

            OWNER               ===> texts      Userid or group name
            LEVEL               ===> 0          0-99
            FAILED ACCESSES     ===> FAIL       FAIL or WARN
            UACC                ===> NONE       NONE, READ, UPDATE,
                                                CONTROL, ALTER or EXECUTE
```

Figure 6.6 The new 'TEXTS.*.*' profile

Now you can get back to the window where you are logged in as MYUSER. However, before you can use your new privileges, you might need to log on as a member of the TEXTS group. In some cases, a RACF user is treated as a member of only one group at a time (this depends on the system options and is explained in Topic 5.2.6 of *z/OS V1R7.0 Security Server RACF Security Administrator's Guide*).

If you already logged on as MYUSER, log off. Then log on again, entering **TEXTS** as your group, as shown in Figure 6.7.

```
---------------------------- TSO/E LOGON ----------------------------------


    Enter LOGON parameters below:           RACF LOGON parameters:

    Userid    ===> MYUSER                    Seclabel     ===>

    Password  ===>                           New Password ===>

    Procedure ===> GENERAL                   Group Ident  ===> texts
```

Figure 6.7   Log on as a member of TEXTS.

> **Warning**
>
> For performance reasons, user permissions are read when the user logs on. This means that if you revoke a user's access because of an intrusion, real or suspected, you have to log off that user immediately. To do so, go to SDSF, select DA for active users, and issue the line command K (for kill) for the job whose name is the same as the user ID.

Now MYUSER should be able to view the RACF profiles of data sets in the TEXTS group. Run this TSO command to list the data set profiles of that group. If you are running it from ISPF, remember to prefix it with TSO.

```
LISTDSD PREFIX(TEXTS)
```

To see that the rights of MYUSER are limited, try to read the group profile for TEXTS and then the group profile for a different group, such as SYS1:

```
LISTGRP TEXTS
LISTGRP SYS1
```

The results should be similar to those shown in Figure 6.8.

```
listgrp texts
 INFORMATION FOR GROUP TEXTS
     SUPERIOR GROUP=SYS1        OWNER=ORIPOME
     NO INSTALLATION DATA
     NO MODEL DATA SET
     TERMUACC
     NO SUBGROUPS
     USER(S)=     ACCESS=      ACCESS COUNT=     UNIVERSAL ACCESS=
        MYUSER       USE          000003               NONE
           CONNECT ATTRIBUTES=AUDITOR
           REVOKE DATE=NONE                RESUME DATE=NONE
 READY
listgrp sys1
 ICH32002I NOT AUTHORIZED TO LIST BASE INFORMATION FOR GROUP SYS1
 READY
```

Figure 6.8   MYUSER is authorized to view only some group profiles.

6.2.2 The `group-SPECIAL` Authority

The `group-SPECIAL` authority enables users to do anything with any profile or resource owned by the group and its subgroups and users.

As yourself, the user with SPECIAL permissions, take away MYUSER's `group-AUDITOR` and instead grant that user `group-SPECIAL` on TEXTS. You can do it with this TSO command:

`CONNECT MYUSER GROUP(TEXTS) NOAUDITOR SPECIAL`

As MYUSER, log off and log back on to reset your permissions. MYUSER should now be able to alter the RACF profiles of group resources. To demonstrate this, give MYUSER the ability to read data sets protected by the generic profile you created in the previous section:

`PERMIT 'TEXTS.*.*' GENERIC ACCESS(READ) ID(MYUSER)`

Use the editor to verify that you now have read access to TEXTS.BOOKS.TEXT(DESC), but not update access. Use `cancel` to leave the editor without saving.

> ### Warning
>
> This is not the recommended way to let users manipulate profiles. If you know which profiles the user will need to manipulate in advance, it is even better to just put the user in the ACL of the profile with ALTER access. To let the user create new profiles, connect him or her to the group with CREATE, which lets the user create new profiles owned by the group and automatically grants the user ALTER access to manipulate them.
>
> The `group-SPECIAL` permission is used when it is not known which profiles a user will need to manipulate. For example, this is the permission you would give a group of security administrators who will need to handle all the group's profiles.

Finally, remove MYUSER's `group-SPECIAL` authority. You can do it as MYUSER because that user is currently `group-SPECIAL`:

```
CONNECT MYUSER GROUP(TEXTS) NOSPECIAL
```

After you do this, log off as MYUSER and log on again to reset your permissions. After you log on again, try to give yourself back the special authority and see you fail:

```
CONNECT MYUSER GROUP(TEXTS) SPECIAL
```

6.2.3 The `group-OPERATIONS` Authority

Another group-level authority, `group-OPERATIONS`, enables users to read and update all the data sets that belong to a group. Note that the same functionality is available using ACLs, which is the preferred method.

6.3 System-Level Authorities

Three system-level authorities correspond to the three group-level authorities, except that they apply to all the profiles on a system instead of just those owned by a group or its subgroups.

- **system-AUDITOR**—This authority grants privileges related to auditing. It enables users to specify what information will be audited, to read and delete auditing information, and so on.
- **system-SPECIAL**—This authority is the nearest thing RACF has to a superuser. Users with `system-SPECIAL` can modify profiles to give themselves any permission they do not possess. Your own account, which you've used to manipulate RACF this entire book, has this authority.
- **system-OPERATIONS**—This authority grants the right to read and modify data sets, bypassing the UACC and ACL. As with `group-OPERATIONS`, it is recommended that you use ACLs instead.

> **Warning**
>
> Most z/OS systems are set up so that *very* few user IDs have such strong authorities. In most cases, it is possible to administer RACF using a set of users who have group authorities over parts of the database. This allows enterprises to implement separation of duties, which allows for checks and balances even among the z/OS security administrators.
>
> System-level authorities allow administrators to bypass such checks and balances. Use with caution and only when absolutely necessary.

6.4 Manipulating Users

The previous sections dealt with delegating the capability to view and manipulate data and its protections. Another action that is often delegated is the capability to create and manipulate user accounts.

6.4.1 Creating Users

To create new profiles in RACF, a user must have `CLAUTH`, class authority, for that class (or have an applicable `SPECIAL` authority). For a user who doesn't have `SPECIAL` authority to create new users, the user must fulfill two conditions:

- Have class authority for the class `USER`
- Have `JOIN` group authority for some group

To delegate user creation, modify MYUSER's user profile. You can do it using the following TSO commands:

```
ALTUSER MYUSER CLAUTH(USER)
CONNECT MYUSER GROUP(TEXTS) AUTHORITY(JOIN)
```

Next, log off as MYUSER and log on again to refresh the permissions. At this point, you should be able to create a new user using the same method you used to create MYUSER back in Section 2.1, "Creating a User." Alternatively, you can create a new user using a TSO command:

```
ADDUSER YAUSER PASSWORD(YAUSER) DFLTGRP(TEXTS)
```

Figure 6.9 shows the profile of the new user. You can then view the user's profile because, as the creator, MYUSER is the default owner.

```
listuser yauser
 USER=YAUSER  NAME=UNKNOWN  OWNER=MYUSER    CREATED=07.107
  DEFAULT-GROUP=TEXTS     PASSDATE=00.000  PASS-INTERVAL= 30
  ATTRIBUTES=NONE
  REVOKE DATE=NONE   RESUME DATE=NONE
  LAST-ACCESS=UNKNOWN
  CLASS AUTHORIZATIONS=NONE
  NO-INSTALLATION-DATA
  NO-MODEL-NAME
  LOGON ALLOWED   (DAYS)          (TIME)
  --------------------------------------------------
  ANYDAY                          ANYTIME
   GROUP=TEXTS    AUTH=USE     CONNECT-OWNER=MYUSER    CONNECT-DATE=07.107
    CONNECTS=    00  UACC=NONE    LAST-CONNECT=UNKNOWN
    CONNECT ATTRIBUTES=NONE
    REVOKE DATE=NONE   RESUME DATE=NONE
```

Figure 6.9   The new user created by MYUSER

Now try to create another user whose default group is one where MYUSER does not have join authority—for example, OMVS:

ADDUSER YAUSER2 PASSWORD(YAUSER2) DFLTGRP(OMVS)

It will fail, as shown in Figure 6.10.

```
adduser yauser2 password(yauser2) dfltgrp(omvs)
ICH01011I INSUFFICIENT AUTHORITY.
ICH01010I USER(S) NOT ADDED.
READY
```

Figure 6.10   MYUSER cannot create a user in OMVS.

If you try to log on to TSO with YAUSER, you will fail because YAUSER does not have a TSO segment in the user profile. MYUSER is not allowed to access TSO segments, as you can see in Figure 6.11. The command specifies to show the TSO information and to not show the RACF base information that is shown by default.

```
listuser yauser tso noracf
IRR52021I You are not authorized to view TSO segments.
READY
```

Figure 6.11   MYUSER fails to read the TSO segment of a user profile.

6.4.1.1 Permitting MYUSER Access to the TSO Segment

Permissions for fields inside RACF profiles are explained in *z/OS 1.6 Security Server RACF Security Administrator's Guide,* Topic 7.3, "Field-level Access Checking." Unless a specific profile governs access to TSO segments, only users with system-SPECIAL will be able to modify it.

These commands must be executed by your regular user, the one with system-SPECIAL.

SETROPTS CLASSACT(FIELD)
SETROPTS RACLIST(FIELD)
SETROPTS GENERIC(FIELD)

These commands activate the FIELD class if it is not already activated, make sure that profiles are cached in memory, and activate generic profiles within that class.

RDEFINE FIELD USER.TSO.* UACC(NONE)
PERMIT USER.TSO.* CLASS(FIELD) GENERIC ACCESS(UPDATE) ID(MYUSER)
SETROPTS RACLIST(FIELD) REFRESH

These commands define a generic profile that covers all the fields in the TSO segment of user profiles and grant access to MYUSER. The final command refreshes the cached copy in memory so the change will be effective the next time MYUSER logs on.

> **Warning**
>
> This provides MYUSER with access to the TSO segments for *all* users. RACF has no way to restrict access to users in a particular group.

6.4.1.2 Creating the New TSO Segment

At this point—at least, after you log off and log back on—MYUSER can read the TSO segment of YAUSER's profile, as you can see in Figure 6.12. However, there is no TSO information.

```
listuser yauser tso noracf
USER=YAUSER

NO TSO INFORMATION
READY
```

Figure 6.12   MYUSER reads an empty TSO segment.

At this point, MYUSER can specify that TSO procedure for YAUSER. In most cases, this is GENERAL:

```
ALTUSER YAUSER TSO(PROC(GENERAL))
```

Now YAUSER should be able to log on TSO.

> **Note**
>
> New accounts are always created with expired passwords. The first time YAUSER logs on, he or she will have to change to a new password.

6.4.2 Manipulating Users

Several profiles in the `FACILITY` class enable users to manipulate existing user profiles. These profiles give permissions only to manipulate regular users. They do not apply to users with any of the three administrative authorities: `AUDITOR`, `SPECIAL`, and `OPERATIONS`.

- **IRR.LISTUSER**—The capability to list user information
- **IRR.PASSWORD.RESET**—The capability to reset passwords
- **IRR.DIGTCERT.****—Permissions to manage digital certificates

To demonstrate the first two profiles, run these commands as your own user to give permissions to YAUSER.

First, verify that the `FACILITY` class is active. Run this command:

```
SETROPTS LIST
```

The `FACILITY` class is probably active, as shown in Figure 6.13.

```
setropts list
 ATTRIBUTES = INITSTATS WHEN(PROGRAM -- BASIC) SAUDIT CMDVIOL NOOPERAUDIT
 STATISTICS = NONE
 AUDIT CLASSES = DATASET DIRACC UNIXPRIV
 ACTIVE CLASSES = DATASET USER GROUP ACCTNUM CBIND CIMS DIMS FACILITY FIELD
                  FSSEC GXFACILI LOGSTRM PTKTDATA PTKTVAL RODMMGR SCDMBR
                  SECDATA SECLABEL SECLMBR SERVER STARTED TSOAUTH TSOPROC
                  UNIXPRIV XFACILIT
```

Figure 6.13   FACILITY class active

If it is not active, run this command:

```
SETROPTS CLASSACT(FACILITY)
```

Next, see if you have the top two profiles:

```
RLIST FACILITY IRR.LISTUSER
RLIST FACILITY IRR.PASSWORD.RESET
```

These profiles probably do not exist, as shown in Figure 6.14.

```
rlist facility irr.listuser
 ICH13003I IRR.LISTUSER NOT FOUND
 READY
rlist facility irr.password.reset
 ICH13003I IRR.PASSWORD.RESET NOT FOUND
 READY
```

Figure 6.14   The user-manipulation profiles do not exist.

If the profiles do not exist, use these commands to create them:

```
RDEFINE FACILITY IRR.LISTUSER UACC(NONE)
RDEFINE FACILITY IRR.PASSWORD.RESET UACC(NONE)
```

Next, create the ACL entries and refresh the RACF cache.

```
PERMIT IRR.LISTUSER CLASS(FACILITY) ACCESS(READ) ID(YAUSER)
PERMIT IRR.PASSWORD.RESET CLASS(FACILITY) ACCESS(READ) ID(YAUSER)
SETROPTS REFRESH RACFLIST(FACILITY)
```

To see the entries with the ACLs, run these commands:

```
RLIST FACILITY IRR.LISTUSER ALL
RLIST FACILITY IRR.PASSWORD.RESET ALL
```

To verify that this works, log on as YAUSER and try to list MYUSER and change its password.

```
LISTUSER MYUSER
ALTUSER MYUSER PASSWORD(MYUSER)
```

This will work. However, if you try to do the same thing with your own user, it will fail because your own user has administrative privileges, as shown in Figure 6.15.

```
altuser myuser password(myuser)
 READY
altuser oripome password(oripome)
 ICH21005I NOT AUTHORIZED TO SPECIFY PASSWORD/NOPASSWORD, OPERAND IGNORED.
 READY
listuser oripome
 ICH30002I NOT AUTHORIZED TO LIST ORIPOME
 READY
listuser myuser
 USER=MYUSER  NAME=SAMPLE USER              OWNER=ORIPOME   CREATED=07.016
  DEFAULT-GROUP=OMVS       PASSDATE=00.000  PASS-INTERVAL= 30
  ATTRIBUTES=NONE
  REVOKE DATE=NONE   RESUME DATE=NONE
```

Figure 6.15   User-manipulation profiles do not affect users with administrative authority on RACF.

These permissions are appropriate for people who need to administer users but do not have permission to create new users, such as service desk employees.

This concludes the hands-on part of this book. At this point, you should be able to create users, authorize them, log their actions, audit the system, and delegate administrative privileges to other users. You are still far from being a mainframe security expert, but you should also know where to go for more information.

The final chapter of this book is more theoretical. It explains, in broad details, how to build an integrated security infrastructure for an enterprise and how mainframes fit into such infrastructure.

6.5 Additional Information

- *z/OS Security Server RACF Security Administrator's Guide,* which explains the use of groups and inheritance, as well as the three authorities (AUDITOR, SPECIAL, OPERATIONS) and the use of FACILITY class profiles
- *z/OS Security Server RACF Command Language Reference,* which explains the commands used in this chapter

Mainframes in the Enterprise-Wide Security Infrastructure

Until now, we have discussed how to interact with a z/OS system and how to administer users, set permissions, and collect and view audit reports on a z/OS system. In this chapter, we look beyond the z/OS system to understand how security capabilities on z/OS work in combination with security capabilities on other systems and security components in a heterogeneous computing environment.

This chapter reviews the concept of an enterprise and what comprises an enterprise. It introduces security functions that span an enterprise (end-to-end security). It also reviews several commonly used communications protocols and how they are used to communicate with applications running on z/OS systems and information stored on them. All these characteristics impact how end-to-end security is configured and used within an enterprise.

This chapter covers enterprise-wide security administration, enterprise authentication and authorization (access control) configurations, and credential propagation and transform processing used to avoid reauthentication of users interacting with systems in the enterprise. We close this chapter with a discussion on cross-enterprise security and how to pass credentials between cooperating partners over the Internet.

Because of the topic, this chapter has to be different from the rest of the book. RACF is a specific system that performs similar functions on all mainframes where it is installed. This similarity enabled us to explain exact steps and commands that would work for all readers of this book. On the other hand, enterprise-wide security infrastructures vary enormously among enterprises. Some enterprises use manual account provisioning, some use home-grown scripts, and some use IBM Tivoli Identity Manager. Some enterprises protect their web-based applications on the web servers, some use IBM Tivoli Access Manager, and some use a mixture of both. It would be impossible to describe the commands and methods used by all the enterprises within the scope of this book. Therefore, this chapter is a high-level architectural view of the tasks that an enterprise-wide security infrastructure performs. For exact details about the implementation in your enterprise, you will need to ask a knowledgeable security administrator or read the local documentation.

7.1 What Is an Enterprise?

Organizations that use computers employ a wide range of methods of procuring, configuring, and managing these systems. Some organizations contract with specialists or services groups to manage the systems they own. Other organizations contract with services groups to provide both the systems and the management of those systems.

In this chapter, we define an enterprise as systems that are used by an organization and within the organization to support the organization's business. This includes server systems in server rooms (including z/OS systems), networking equipment and communications links between sites, network appliances that serve a variety of specialized functions, desktop terminals of whatever form is appropriate for the organization (e.g., point-of-sale terminals, dedicated workstations, or hand-held devices), and any storage systems in both disk and tape formats. The collection of these systems, networks, and storage devices makes up the enterprise for any organization. Figure 7.1 shows a number of enterprises connected to the Internet.

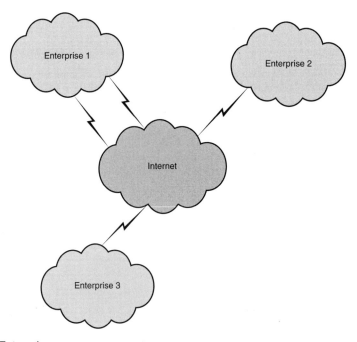

Figure 7.1   Enterprises

The organization's employees or customers might use these systems. The direct use of these systems by an organization's customers has become an accepted and necessary part of an organization's enterprise computing and has drastically expanded the complexity of securing all the systems used in the enterprise, including z/OS. In the past, employees of an organization used z/OS systems (through customer-service applications or back-office applications). Now the same systems are used to service requests from an organization's customers without an intermediate employee of the company serving as an arbiter between the enterprise and the customer.

Later sections in this chapter show how a combination of systems and applications running in the enterprise can securely and accurately track requests from an organization's customers as those requests are handled.

7.1.1 Enterprise Components

As discussed in the previous section, many components come together to construct an enterprise computing environment. Each of these must be installed, configured, customized, and maintained. Furthermore, every device in the enterprise needs to be monitored so that an organization understands the types of devices used and how those devices are being used. Figure 7.2 shows an enterprise with multiple components.

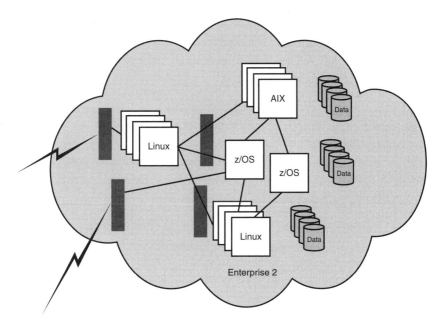

Figure 7.2   The components of an enterprise

In many environments, systems are used as "hosting platforms" for various applications to run. When a new application is to be installed and configured, new systems are often deployed to run those applications, thereby dedicating those systems to be used for just that single application. Although this builds a level of isolation between applications, the methodology also tends to cause a proliferation of systems, some of which are used much more than others. This results in systems that stand idle while other systems are constrained for resources (memory, disk, I/O, etc.) to keep up with the load of requests.

From a security perspective, these dedicated systems (often Linux, UNIX, or Windows server systems) utilize a strict separation between user IDs defined to the operating system and user definitions defined to the application running on the operating system. This is especially prevalent in web server and web application server deployments in which the user registry that the application server uses is typically very different from the user registry defined to the operating system. User IDs on the operating system are meant for administrative work on the system or for user IDs that represent the application server itself (separate and distinct from the users who interact with the application server).

On z/OS, the typical configuration is the opposite. Over many years, organizations have built the user registry on their z/OS systems as the union of administrative users, application server (sometimes referred to as resource manager) user IDs, and user IDs representing people within the organization (employees and contractors/partners of the organization). In this way, the security processing on z/OS serves multiple users and must handle a variety of requests. Although this at first seems more complex, having security definitions for multiple "layers" of the computing environment in one location is beneficial. One benefit is that this provides easier, more coordinated administration of all these security definitions, using a common set of interfaces for administering over the security definitions.

Note

A similar situation exists on many multiuser UNIX systems. Systems contain a few administrative users, such as root, some application server users (daemon users in UNIX terminology) such as httpd, and regular users.

Unlike many other systems, z/OS systems are used to host multiple, concurrent applications and application-serving environments. z/OS contains sophisticated load-balancing support to ensure that computing resources (memory, CPU, and I/O) are directed to those applications that are in greatest need of each resource. This results in higher overall CPU usage percentages without proliferation of an ever-increasing number of server system footprints.

An enterprise often consists of a combination of Linux, UNIX, and Windows systems along with several z/OS "transaction server" systems. Added to this are myriad networking devices, from firewalls, routers, and wireless access points, to load balancers, cryptographic accelerators, and virtual private networking (VPN) appliances. On z/OS, many organizations run a combination of Customer Information Control System (CICS®), Information Management System (IMS™), WebSphere® MQ (messaging and queuing), and database management systems (e.g., DB2 Universal Database for z/OS). z/OS systems are also used to host other application-serving environments, including web servers and web application servers (e.g., WebSphere Application Server), as well as directory and security servers such as LDAP directory servers and Kerberos Key Distribution Centers (KDCs).

When applications are deployed on smaller server platforms, these applications are typically isolated from one another by deploying new systems for each application. Alternatively, applications and application servers running on z/OS run alongside other applications and application servers. The difference in scope of the z/OS security registry relative to other systems' user registries results in several interesting challenges (and solutions) in accomplishing end-to-end security across the enterprise. We explore this subject in greater detail later in this chapter.

7.1.2 Security across Enterprise Components

Although the use of multiple systems and system types across the enterprise creates a challenge for consistent and coordinated administration, such configurations enable organizations to set up highly secure computing systems. One of the basic tenets of setting up secure environments is to utilize the concept of "layers of defense," as shown in Figure 7.3. By building a system with multiple layers of security checking before an undesirable action is taken, it is less likely that the action will be performed.

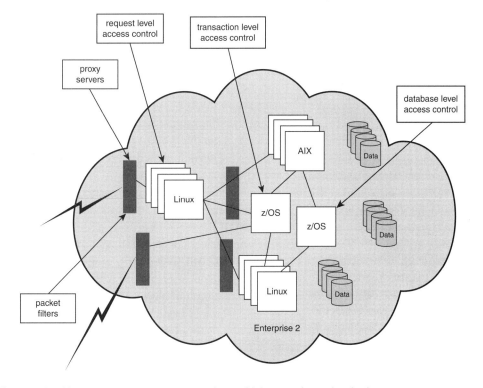

Figure 7.3 Heterogeneous systems require multiple security technologies.

By building a computing environment that has these multiple layers of defense, an organization can be more confident that its corporate assets will not be misused or tampered with by outside or inside attackers. If multiple layers of defense are not employed, organizations typically have weak points in their security configurations that lend themselves to an attack. Many organizations consider the information and processing that is performed within the computing environment as their most valued corporate assets. And often this information and processing is hosted on a complex of z/OS systems running within their enterprise.

Multiple diverse technologies are used to build these layers of defense across an enterprise. Typically, the outer layers of defense revolve around constraining communications into the enterprise from outside and even among various networking zones (physical/logical areas within the enterprise). Networking security is built using several technologies, including firewalls, intelligent network routers, proxy servers, and packet-filtering appliances. These devices and systems build a first layer of defense for the enterprise, effectively filtering out, at the networking level, communications that are deemed potentially dangerous or suspected attacks. Examples of this type of operation are network filters that can be set up to disallow any communications through those filters except TCP/IP communications over port 80 (designated for HTTP) to a designated HTTP proxy with a specific IP address. This HTTP proxy might further filter the HTTP requests to allow only those requests that it deems valid to pass on to an HTTP server, which can then respond to the request.

Access control (also referred to as authorization) is then used in multiple areas of the enterprise to form additional layers of defense around the enterprise's information and applications. By using multiple layers of access control, organizations can ensure proper use and protect against misuse of their information and processing capacity, even when these applications and databases are accessed through a diverse set of paths; these might include requests from outside the enterprise (from an organization's customers and partners), requests from within the enterprise (through applications that the organization's employees and contractors use), and operations by the administrative staff (through commands, operations, and procedures that the system administrators use to keep the enterprise operating, secure, and backed up).

HTTP proxy servers running in the computing environment can apply access control for each request (request-level access control). These checks ensure that the requester is allowed to make the request that was passed into the environment. If the request appears valid, the application/transaction often performs additional access-control checks, using additional context and information found within the request, to determine whether the requester is allowed to invoke the transaction. If all the checks are approved, the transaction is performed. With widely distributed applications, it is quite common for multiple transactions to be invoked as part of processing a single incoming request and for a transaction to be invoked from several different requests.

Correctly defining the access controls at the transaction level can be a difficult task because the alignment among applications, external requests, and transactions is often quite complex.

Even after transaction-level access controls are applied, additional access checking at the file or database level can offer yet another layer of defense. This layer of defense is often used to ensure that only a user defined on the specific system (possibly the user ID under which the application server environment is running) is allowed to access the information held on the system.

Recall from the previous section that it is quite common for z/OS systems to have user definitions for employees of the organization who are using the applications served by the enterprise. Because of this, and because such environments have been built up over many years, these employees have been granted access to databases, files, and transactions running on the z/OS system. An organization often needs to ensure that the access controls that have been put in place on the z/OS systems continue to be used even when new applications, running on different systems but used by the same employees of the organization, are provided to these employees. Furthermore, when applications and services are provided to the organization's customers or partners, similar access controls need to be set up at each of these layers of defense to ensure consistent access to these resources (files, databases, and transactions).

Building an enterprise containing multiple layers of defense is a challenge. However, to ensure that the resources served by the enterprise are used as intended, these multiple layers of defense are necessary. The task for enterprise security administrators is to deploy and configure these layers of defense so that the right people are allowed to perform the right tasks with the right amount of access-control checking and auditing applied as requests flow from system to system and environment to environment across the enterprise.

7.1.3 Communication Protocols

When employees who connected directly to z/OS systems through "green-screen" interfaces accessed mainframe transaction systems such as the Information Management System (IMS) and Customer Information Control System (CICS), only a couple protocols were required. Terminal emulator software, running on desktop computers, allowed for direct 3270 (LU 2) protocol communication with the z/OS system, and users authenticated directly to the z/OS system to use its applications. Today, these same transaction systems are used at the core of many enterprise-computing environments. However, the communications protocols used between the end user (employee, customer, or partner) and the transaction systems vary widely; in many cases, multiple protocols are employed among multiple proxy, appliance, and application-server environments as requests travel from an end user to the transaction servers that handle these requests. The communications protocols used across the enterprise are important to understand because these protocols dictate networking requirements such as firewall configuration. These protocols also determine the sets and types of credential formats that can be used between communicating parts of the enterprise. A credential is information that represents the authenticated identity of the user making the request.

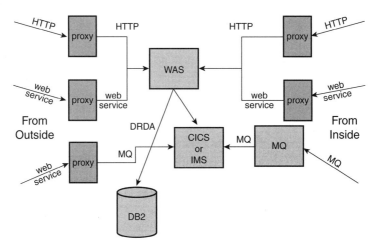

Figure 7.4   Communication protocols transfer security information.

The communications protocol with the most explosive growth, due to the popularity and usefulness of the Internet, is the Hyper Text Transfer Protocol (HTTP). This protocol enables HTTP "browsers" to send requests to HTTP "servers," allowing interaction by a user with whatever is running on the HTTP server. HTTP began as a means for delivering information to users (thus the term *browser* on the requester side). HTTP is now used to convey very expressive, interactive user interfaces, making applications that are isolated available within an enterprise, as well as enabling applications to be "customer facing" or accessible from outside the enterprise. Figure 7.4 shows that the same application servers and transaction servers are often used to handle requests coming from both internal (enterprise) applications and customer-facing (Internet) applications. Because of the capabilities of the HTTP protocol, its popularity, and the pervasiveness of high-function "browsers," HTTP is often the first protocol through which transaction requests pass in today's computing environments. HTTP protocol requests contain header and content information within requests. Security information about the requester and server often flows in customized fields in the HTTP headers, enabling both requester and responder to understand who is requesting the information or service.

Emerging as the next generation of protocol used to convey requests and responses, both over the Internet and within organizations, is the web service. A web service is most often built as an extension that rides on top of the HTTP protocol and consists of a specially designed definition of the information that flows within the content area of HTTP protocol requests and responses. Web services often use the Simple Object Application Protocol (SOAP) over HTTP. SOAP requests and responses have been standardized to include extensible security header fields that are more structured than HTTP header fields. Furthermore, certain formulations of security information in SOAP headers have been standardized to allow for interoperability between communicating partners, enabling organizations to separate the implementations of requester and server while still enabling the secure conveyance of who is requesting the information or service.

HTTP, through a browser, is used for end-user interactions. Web services are used when programs communicate with one another.

An enterprise uses a wide variety of additional protocols. As communications come closer to applications running on z/OS, these protocols become more streamlined to enable fast communications and fast response to requests passed in. Many z/OS applications are accessible using Message Queuing (MQ) interfaces. Message Queuing is a form of communications in which the sender/requester puts a message onto a queue and then waits for a response via a message on a response queue. Such processing enables a separation of requester and responder, and also enables asynchronous handling of requests. MQ interfaces exist as a way of communicating between application servers as well as with transaction servers, such as IMS and CICS. Note that MQ messages have a header section (where security-relevant attributes about the requester are located) as well as a message payload (where parameters or response information for the request are passed).

Some enterprises employ transaction server-specific protocols. Two examples of these are Open Transaction Manager Access (OTMA), used to communicate with an IMS transaction server running on z/OS, and External CICS Interface (EXCI), used to communicate with a CICS transaction server running on z/OS. Both of these protocols flow over TCP/IP communications links and enable invocation of IMS and CICS transactions, respectively. Both of these protocols define specific security-relevant fields in their protocol definitions and, thus, constrain the types of security information that can be passed into IMS and CICS.

In addition to transaction server-specific protocols for transaction servers, another protocol, defined by the Distributed Relational Database Architecture™ (DRDA®) is used to communicate directly with relational database management systems (DBMSs). DRDA also defines specific security information fields that can be used to convey who is requesting the DBMS to perform the operation, supplied within the DRDA protocol request.

Many enterprises use distributed object applications that conform to the Java 2 Enterprise Edition (J2EE) specification. Distributed object communications typically flow over a protocol called Remote Method Invocation/Internet Inter-Orb Protocol (RMI/IIOP). This protocol contains an extensible security section within which information about the requester of the remote method invocation is passed.

In most enterprises, the applications the employees, customers, and partners use have been built over time with incremental enhancements from release to release of these applications. The net result of this process is that requests commonly pass through multiple communications systems across the enterprise, with various protocols used between communicating entities. An external-facing HTTP proxy (HTTP protocol) might communicate with an application server, which, in turn, communicates with a set of J2EE Enterprise Java Beans (EJBs) using RMI/IIOP.

Those EJBs might then communicate with CICS transactions on z/OS using the EXCI protocol. Or the EJBs might use MQ messages to invoke IMS transactions. Or the application server might use DRDA to make direct database requests to a DB2 DBMS running on z/OS. In every case, the authenticated identity (credentials) corresponding to the original requester (or some identity representing the requester) must flow to each computing system so that proper access controls (those layers of defense) can be properly utilized. Later in this chapter, we discuss this credential transfer and transform in more detail.

7.2 Enterprise Security Administration

Across the enterprise, multiple security systems commonly are employed by the wide variety of platforms and applications. This multiplicity of security systems, built over years of evolution of the enterprise, now presents a challenge for organizations to administer in a coordinated, consistent manner. The set of user and group definitions in each of these security systems represents a subset of the overall set of users and groups defined to be capable of interacting with the enterprise in some way.

Administration of user and group information in RACF databases across multiple z/OS systems is part of this administration work. RACF administration must be coordinated with updates made to other enterprise user and group registries so that people and applications represented by the user IDs are able to access and interact with only their allowed systems and applications.

Enterprise administration refers to the capability to manage RACF information alongside other user registries, such as Lightweight Directory Access Protocol (LDAP)–accessible directories, e-mail systems, and UNIX systems. Ideally, administration of users is done based on a person's job function or the roles that person plays within the organization.

Tools such as IBM Tivoli Identity Manager and IBM Tivoli Directory Integrator offer the capability to administer multiple security systems across the enterprise in a policy-based manner. This enables organizations to concentrate on the roles and job functions of their employees and the set of permissions those roles require. Administering users in a policy-based manner frees administrators from the burden of entering, in a repeatable manner, user-specific permissions settings; instead, administrators can deploy a role-based access control (RBAC) model. With an RBAC model in place, organizations are less dependent on individual user permissions and are better able to articulate the capabilities that people have within the organization—more important, they can better define why they have such capabilities based on the roles each person can play.

When performing administration at the enterprise level, it is important to manage the multitude of user and group registries in a coordinated manner to ensure consistency across the enterprise.

7.2.1 Authentication and Authorization

After users are defined to the multiple security systems that comprise security for the enterprise, users have the ability to authenticate themselves to various applications running within the enterprise. Such authentication should be performed "at the edge" of a user's interaction with the enterprise (whether at a login prompt on a desktop of a notebook computer or at some login prompt used to access an enterprise portal environment through which multiple applications are made accessible).

To streamline employees' use of the enterprise, users should not be reprompted for the same authenticating information when they communicate with multiple underlying servers or systems upon which the applications are hosted. Sometimes referred to as single sign-on (SSO), the capability to reuse credentials acquired during an initial login processing greatly simplifies a user's interaction with enterprise applications. Operating this way requires that this authenticating information be passed from application to application and system to system across the enterprise. As discussed in Section 7.1.3, "Communication Protocols," the authenticating information (credentials) that can be passed between communicating entities is limited by the capabilities of the communications protocol used between those communicating entities.

It is quite possible that several credential transformations will be used as requests flow from one part of the enterprise to be handled by an application running in another part of the enterprise. When credentials are transformed, two benefits emerge: Precise access controls already in place and applicable to the requester can be applied or enforced, and audit log information can indicate the specific requester of the processing. Because multiple-authorization-checking policy enforcement points (PEPs) are likely to exist along the path that an application request takes, multiple credential transformations might be necessary as the request crosses the enterprise for processing.

Enterprise security authentication and authorization implement the layers of defense that users must get through for the enterprise to process their requests.

7.2.2 Credential Propagation and Transformation

Previous sections described the topics of cross-enterprise security administration, authentication at the edge of the enterprise, and authorization at multiple policy enforcement points (PEPs) across the enterprise. Central to enabling such constructs to be implemented in an independent and layered fashion across an enterprise is the capability to associate user and group definitions across user registries and to transform credentials into formats that are useful on the systems and over the protocols that are used in implementing applications that cross multiple systems and networks, including z/OS.

Enterprise user administration systems implicitly hold association between user definitions in separate user registries. These systems must maintain which user IDs are assigned to which people and applications in the enterprise. This association is critical for performing coordinated administration of user and group definitions across the enterprise. This association is also required for credential transformations as application request processing flows from one computing system to another in handling the end user's requests.

As was described in the section on communications protocols and credentials, the credentials used over the protocols are often not in a format that enables PEPs on the computing systems to invoke access control checks. A transformation of credentials, from the format used over the protocol into the format required by the access control checking function, must be performed. Products such as IBM Tivoli Federated Identity Manager help organizations set up, configure, and maintain credential transformation as a callable service available to multiple parts of the enterprise. Figure 7.5 shows an example application request flow as the request starts from a user and moves through elements that process the request. At each point in the processing is a layer of defense in the form of access control checks. However, the access control checking function expects user information to be supplied in a form that is specific to each system used in building enterprise applications.

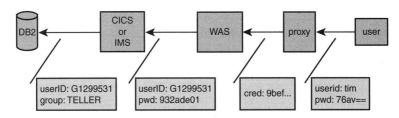

Figure 7.5   Credential propagation example within an enterprise

In the example, the user initially authenticates using a user ID and password combination that flows over HTTP basic authentication fields defined by the HTTP protocol. An intervening proxy is able to verify the user ID and password combination (based on the user registry that the proxy is configured to use). The proxy builds an internal credential to be used for URL-level access control checks. Before the request is passed on to the next system to be used to handle the request (assuming that the access control check determines that the user is allowed to invoke the operation), the proxy must transform the user credentials into a format that is acceptable for the protocol over which the request will pass—as well as one that is acceptable to the application server listening for requests over that protocol.

The proxy in the example transforms the credentials used for the request into a format that the application server (WebSphere Application Server—WAS) and proxy server have mutually agreed to use. The figure indicates that a private format represented by the name "cred:" is used; in this case, this is a binary formulation of user identity and group membership (abbreviated by "9bef…" in Figure 7.5). The application server receives the request and transforms the incoming credential format into a form that is usable by the access-control checking function used by the application server. Access checks in the application server represent the next layer of defense for allowing the user to invoke the request that has been made.

In the example, the application server contacts a CICS (or IMS) transaction server to handle part of the original request made by the user. Here the CICS (or IMS) transaction server was contacted using protocols that require information about the requester to be passed in various formats. In the example, a user ID and password combination has been selected, in which the user ID is a valid user ID on the system on which the CICS (or IMS) transaction server is running (in many cases, this is a RACF database on the z/OS system in which CICS [or IMS] is running). Again, a credential transform operation is required to establish which user ID (and password) to use as the credential passed to CICS (or IMS). In the case of RACF, a one-time password formulation called a passticket can be used, alleviating the need to hold password vaults or store password values in configuration files.

When the CICS (or IMS) transaction server receives the request, RACF verifies the user ID and password or passticket, and an operating system–specific credential format called an ACEE is constructed. This ACEE travels with the request processing on the z/OS system and passes to other subsystems on z/OS (such as DB2) so that access control checks within those subsystems can use the information about the requester of the processing. These access control checks in the transaction server and database server represent additional layers of defense for the enterprise application.

Several algorithms can be used for credential transformation. Those algorithms can be categorized by their user-mapping characteristics:

- **1:1**—For any incoming user definition, find a corresponding user definition in the target user registry. Each incoming user ID has a unique user ID in the target user registry that is to be selected.

- **Many:1**—For any incoming user definition, use a single configured user definition as the user ID to send to the next layer of processing.

- **Many:some**—For any incoming user definition, determine, based on user characteristics or environmental information, a representative user ID in the target user registry to use. The target user ID might be chosen based on the application that is being used, based on the group or organizational unit that the user is a part of or some combination of other factors (e.g., time of day, connection method).

In enterprise applications, initial authentication, credential transform, layers of defense, and security administration must be set up in a coordinated manner across the enterprise. Access control checks across multiple systems in the enterprise form these layers of defense. Enterprise security administration based on the associations between user IDs held in separate security registries ensures that these layers of defense have appropriate user definitions that requests can utilize. Credential transform uses these security associations so that application processing and requests can transfer the necessary credentials between communicating partners as requests are processed.

7.3 Communicating between Enterprises—and Beyond

Organizations are no longer using their computing systems only in isolated enterprise environments. Enterprises are connected to the Internet to allow for customers' direct use of an organization's computing systems through "web-facing" applications. Also, organizations often contract with service providers to provide various types of computing functions, such as backup services, employee benefits processing, employee travel services, etc. Figure 7.6 illustrates this.

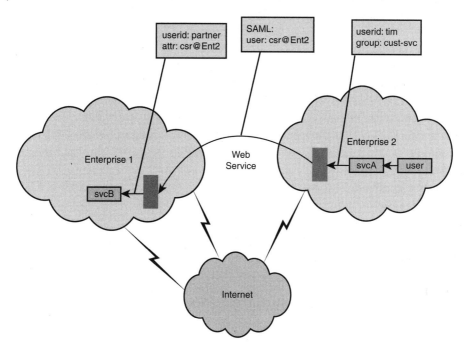

Figure 7.6   Credential propagation between enterprises

The same types of problems shown in the previous section occur when enterprises open up their operations to allow customers to invoke processing on their computing systems, as well as when enterprises contract for using services provided by some service provider. In all cases, enterprises need to accept user credentials over some communications protocol, transform these credentials into something that can be used within the enterprise, perform access control checks on requests, handle them, and log that these requests have been requested and performed.

Although the pattern for processing is the same, the types of credentials used and the transformations required differ. In the case of sending requests between communicating partners (either from customers or with partner organizations), standards-based formats such as web services (communicated using the Simple Object Access Protocol [SOAP]) are commonly used to convey requests. Also, standards-based credential formats such as Security Assertion Markup Language (SAML) are used within SOAP requests to convey requester credential information.

Standardized credential formats are used between organizations. These formats are usually transformed into formats based on user registries defined within the enterprise as the request is received and processed within the enterprise. The standard formats and the credential transformations enable organizations to isolate the credential formats and user registries used internally from those used between enterprises. Such layers of isolation enable independent change and upgrade of computing environments, while still supporting the same form of external interfaces. Isolation also enables existing credential formats to be used internally, thereby enabling existing applications to be used without requiring massivechanges to these applications.

In this chapter, we discussed how z/OS systems that utilize RACF can be used as a part of enterprise applications that make use of computing resources running on multiple, heterogeneous systems across an enterprise. We also discussed how such cross-enterprise processing uses multiple protocols to convey requests between communicating partners, and we stated that credential transformations are required to establish a user's credentials in the required formats so that requests can flow among systems within the enterprise. We also showed how request processing between organizations and enterprises is similar to such processing within an enterprise; the difference is the credential formats and protocols used for communication. By implementing security administration, authentication, authorization, and credential transform capabilities across the enterprise, including RACF and z/OS systems, an organization can apply its many computing resources across the enterprise in a coordinated manner.

7.4 Additional Information

- "Understanding SOA Security Design and Implementation," IBM Redbook SG24-7310, www.redbooks.ibm.com/abstracts/sg247310.html?Open

- "Enterprise Security Architecture Using IBM Tivoli Security Solutions," IBM Redbook SG24-6014, www.redbooks.ibm.com/redpieces/abstracts/sg246014.html?Open

- LDAP on z/OS manuals

- TFIM manuals

- Redbook on patterns: "Connecting Apps to the Enterprise," www.redbooks.ibm.com/pubs/pdfs/redbooks/sg246572.pdf

- *CICS—CICS Transaction Gateway*, www.ibm.com/servers/eserver/design_center/websphere_cics.pdf

- *IMS—IMS Connector for Java*, www.ibm.com/software/data/db2imstools/imstools/imsjavcon.html

- *IMS Connect*, www.ibm.com/software/data/db2imstools/imstools/imsconnect.html

- *WebSphere MQ CICS and IMS Bridges*, http://publibfp.boulder.ibm.com/epubs/pdf/csqsav03.pdf

- *WebSphere MQ Application Programming Reference,* http://publibfp.boulder.ibm.com/epubs/html/csqzak09/csqzak09tfrm.htm
- *Tivoli Access Manager Command Reference,* http://publib.boulder.ibm.com/tividd/td/ITAME/GC32-1107-00/en_US/PDF/GC32-1107-00.pdf
- *Tivoli Access Manager Java API Reference,* http://publib.boulder.ibm.com/tividd/td/ITAME/SC32-1141-00/en_US/PDF/SC32-1141-00.pdf

Index

THIS BOOK IS SAFARI ENABLED

INCLUDES FREE 45-DAY ACCESS TO THE ONLINE EDITION

The Safari® Enabled icon on the cover of your favorite technology book means the book is available through Safari Bookshelf. When you buy this book, you get free access to the online edition for 45 days.

Safari Bookshelf is an electronic reference library that lets you easily search thousands of technical books, find code samples, download chapters, and access technical information whenever and wherever you need it.

TO GAIN 45-DAY SAFARI ENABLED ACCESS TO THIS BOOK:

- Go to **http://www.prenhallprofessional.com/safarienabled**

- Complete the brief registration form

- Enter the coupon code found in the front of this book on the "Copyright" page

If you have difficulty registering on Safari Bookshelf or accessing the online edition, please e-mail customer-service@safaribooksonline.com.

PRENTICE
HALL